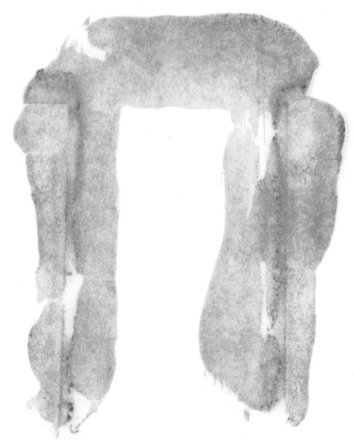

FOR THIS CROSS I'LL KILL YOU

FOR THIS CROSS I'LL KILL YOU

by
BRUCE OLSON

CREATION HOUSE
CAROL STREAM, ILLINOIS

FIRST EDITION

Library of Congress Catalog Number: 73-81494
International Standard Book Number: 0-88419-038-2

To

BOBARISHORA

who passed away while this book

was being born.

The names of persons have been changed where personal embarrassment might be involved.

CONTENTS

Foreword

This book has been a long time in the making. There have been more than a few starts, and we wondered at times whether it could be finished. Somehow it has. This is a tribute to the effect that Bruce Olson has had on all of us.

Bruce is not immediately impressive: tall, slender, blond, with sharp Norwegian features. He is somewhat shy. His speech—always intense—is sometimes staccato, sometimes groping.

He looks very young.

It is hard to match this description with the accolades accorded him. Everyone who meets Bruce regards him with respect; sometimes with awe. After all, at thirty—in spite of having finished college only through correspondence courses—he has spoken to the United Nations and to the Organization of American States. He has lunched with the Vice President of the United States, and has been a close personal friend of the last four presidents of Colombia.

He speaks fifteen languages, has had papers published in linguistic journals, and has pioneered in computer translation of tribal languages.

On top of all this, Bruce Olson has lived alone for more than ten years with the Motilones, a South American tribe which had achieved the dubious distinction of killing almost every outsider who set foot on their territory. Bruce "tied into" the Motilones, and as a result, the Motilones "tied into" God. They also have enjoyed the fastest economic growth of any primitive group in the world—a tribute to Bruce's missionary philosophy which enabled them to retain their basic cultural patterns.

These are just a few of the facts about Bruce Olson. But there is more than these facts would indicate, for no one can spend time with Bruce and remain quite the same. The ideas, the seeds of action which he planted at Creation

House during the few weeks he was with us, continue to affect us, our relationship with each other—and the way we look at ourselves.

Bruce is not impressed with himself. Nor is he concerned about what others think of him or of his work. His drive is not always easy to live with, and Bruce has grated on more than a few people. Consequently he often has been rejected by men. But he hasn't been rejected by God. This is the source of his strength.

We all can learn from him.

The Editors

Creation House

1

Home to the Jungle

Bobby and I found Ayaboquina, a Motilone Indian chieftain, alone in the jungle clearing at the top of the bluff. Green banana shoots and yucca sprouts already were breaking through the ground, and there was plenty of space for cattle grazing on the fifty-five acres. As we talked with Ayaboquina about the progress the Indians were making, we heard a motorboat on the river below. It was too close to the bank for us to see, but we heard it pull in. Usually it takes several minutes for someone to get up to the clearing, but well before we expected it, a swarthy-faced man appeared.

"Good afternoon," he said roughly in Spanish.

He was out of breath and waited impatiently as I continued to speak with Ayaboquina. I saw out of the corner of my eye that it was Humberto Abril, one of the outlaws who had settled the area. I knew he had a bad temper and had threatened the Motilones. Now he obviously was angry.

When I concluded my conversation with Ayaboquina, I said, "Good afternoon, Humberto."

He was sweating heavily, big drops falling from his hollow-cheeked face which was contorted into a shape that made me uneasy.

"I've come to tell you to get off this land," he said. "This is my land. I'm a Colombian colonist. I have the right to claim land for colonization, and I claim this land. You can get off . . ."

He spoke to me, but Bobby interrupted him. "And I have something to tell you." He spoke slowly, calmly, but with great force. "This is our land. It has always been our land. It always will be our land. We have ceded enough land to you. Six months ago we ceded lands to you, at your demand, and what have you done? You have sold them, and now you demand more. But we will not give more. We will protect what is ours."

The argument was short. Humberto began to shake. His neck muscles stood out like steel cords; his face became bright red. He took Bobby by the shoulders and shouted, "These are my lands. They are *mine*. Anyone else must get off." Then he let go of Bobby and stood shaking.

Fear crept up my back like ice. But Bobby was sure of himself. "You are wrong. These lands do not belong to you. They will not belong to you," he said quietly.

"Shut up," Humberto screamed. "Shut up. You dirty Indian, shut up."

Spittle came out of the corners of his mouth and made little spots on his red face. Then he put his forefinger across the thumb of his right hand so that it made a cross. He held it toward us. His eyes bulged and his hand shook so much he could hardly hold it straight. He kissed his fingers.

"For God," he said, kissing his fingers again and spitting on the ground. "For the saints." Again he spit, his head jerking to the side so violently it looked more like a spasm then a conscious movement. "For the Virgin Mother." A third time he spit. "And for this cross." He spit again, then—looking straight at us—he held his thumb and forefinger to his mouth and kissed them. His voice grew gutteral. "I'll kill you!"

Then he screamed it. "I swear, for this cross I'll kill you."

He turned on his heel and walked down the bank. We watched the back of his neck until he disappeared. It was still crimson, and the muscles and veins continued to stand out like cords. We were silent until we heard his boat start up, then fade into the distance.

I was trembling. "Bobby, he will. He will kill. I feel that he means it."

"You are right, Bruchko."

"And what can we do about it?"

Ayaboquina, Bobby and I decided on some safety precautions.

"But, Bruchko," Bobby said, "there is no real safety in these things. Only God can help."

So the three of us bowed our heads and talked to God together. As we did, my fear was replaced by the joy that had seized me when I had first seen Bobby that morning. It crept into my soul, down into my stomach. Yet it was not the same joy. It was more profound, as though pain and danger and fear had been injected into it, making it deeper, warmer, more sensitive.

What a lot had happened in those few hours since my plane had circled the town of Rio de Oro for a landing. Beneath the plane I could see the jungle stretching to the horizon, a dense, heavy green mat. To the right, I caught my first glimpse of a dirty brown streak, like a misplaced string across a green carpet. It was the Catatumbo River. We flew over it at the ferry, and I saw the cluster of houses, all fairly new, that comprised the town. It seemed lost in the vast jungle.

But it is growing, I thought.

It occurred to me that just ten years before there had been nothing but high trees blocking the sun, and dense foliage underneath. Perhaps a parrot had screeched at me. Now, in that same place, was a town.

A flush of joy engulfed me, not because of the town, but because I was coming back from America and soon would be reunited with Bobby, my pact-brother. I strained against the window trying to see ahead of the plane, my emotions swelling from my stomach up my back in a shiver.

As the old, worn-out DC3 lost altitude, the trees came so close to the plane's belly it seemed certain that our wheels would hit and send us spinning into the jungle. But suddenly the foliage broke and we were over a clearing—a narrow.long strip cut out of the jungle. We touched down with a thump and a bounce, the brakes straining to keep the big plane on the small runway.

As we taxied to the end of the strip, my eyes hunted the figures standing there for Bobby. I couldn't find him. But going down the ramp, I spotted him a little to one side, his short, heavy-set torso looking powerful and agile even under his loose-fitting red shirt and dark pants. His face was browner than those of the other people waiting, but even from the ramp I could see his white teeth flashing. It was a smile that said, "You are back again, Bruchko, and it is good." He never used my American name, Bruce.

I broke into a run. When I got to him I grabbed him and gave him a true Motilone greeting. We must have made quite a sight: a short dark Indian embracing a tall blond American. But that made no difference to us.

"My brother," I said. "My brother Bobarishora." I called him by his given name, as I always did in solemn moments.

I held him at arm's length. "You look fine," I said. "How is your wife? And your boy? Are they well?"

"My wife is fine, Bobby said. "She's very healthy and happy. And she's extremely pleased to be the mother of a fine, healthy son."

"Then he's all right?"

"Oh, yes. He's fat. You should see him. And he's already moving around the house like a little monkey.

"Come," he added, "We'd better not stand here all day. Let's get your luggage."

As we walked back to the plane where all baggage had to be claimed, Bobby asked, "And how was your business in America?"

I thought of the streams of faces and the endless hotel rooms, every one alike. I shook my head.

"I don't know, Bobby. I guess I got things done that had to be done. But I'm awfully glad to be back."

Bobby chattered about his family. He was as happy as I had remembered him. His dark eyes were bright. I had worried about him after his daughter had died; for quite a few weeks he had been moody, uncommunicative. Now he didn't seem to be able to stop smiling.

After we got the luggage we decided to eat. We went into the town which had been founded directly on the airstrip. Its narrow, gravel streets were crowded with new homes, their unpainted sides still smelling like fresh wood, their tin roofs still bright among the older, palm-leaf house-tops. They were spindly, rickety things, however, that look-ed as though they couldn't stand long.

I hadn't had any food on the plane and Bobby laughed at the way I stuffed myself with Colombian delicacies.

"You'll have a full stomach from now on, Bruchko," he said.

I knew what he meant. For a Motilone, to have a full stomach means more than not to want more food. It means contentedness, satisfaction with life, happiness. He ex-pressed so well the way I felt.

"How is the cattle program going?" I asked.

"It's going very well. Last week I was a little worried about it, because some of the cows in the highlands were sick. In fact, one of them died. I thought I was going to have to do all the work myself of nursing them back to health. But it worked out all right. The chieftains took care of the problem themselves, gave the right medicine and nursed the cows back to health. The cows seem to be fine now, giving lots of milk." He leaned forward with a sly look. "In fact, Bruchko, we had some left over at Iquiacarora, and it was going bad. So we made cheese."

"What? You made cheese? How did you do that?"

He pretended surprise. "Why, we just made it, like a person always makes cheese." Then he burst out laughing. I must have had a perplexed look. "We had the pills that you left with us. So we read the instructions and figured out how to do it. It came out very well. You can have some when we get to Iquiacarora, if it isn't all gone."

I sat back in amazement. Ten years ago Bobby had been only a friendly kid with a wonderful smile. Now he was a leader of his people. Perhaps making cheese wasn't so important by itself. But it indicated that the Motilone were their own people.

"Bobby," I said, "you now are the leader of your people. It is a great responsibility."

He shrugged. "Well, it's not really me. Lots of other men are able now to take my position. And besides, Bruchko, Jesus Christ walks our trails. He knows our ways, and He knows the things we need. As long as we don't try to deceive Him again, He will be our real leader."

I nodded.

"Bruchko," Bobby said, "you should see the schools. They're crowded. Most of the students have already read through the books we translated, and they want more. Especially more of the New Testament. They talk about the things they're learning as though they were discussing a hunt. The old people, too. We'll have to get to work and translate more for them, or they'll give us no peace."

I laughed. "All right. We'll get busy on that as soon as we can. It should go more quickly now that we've gotten most of the difficult words translated."

The prospect of more translating made me happy. For one thing, I learned much from the Bible in doing it. I thought of the word for faith in Motilone, the word that meant to "tie into" God just as a Motilone tied his hammock into the high rafters of his communal home. "Tied into" Jesus we could rest and sleep and sing from far above the ground without fear of falling.

"I am so glad to be back with you, Bobby," I said. "I missed you the whole time I was away. I guess I am just 'tied into' the Motilone people."

"And we are tied into you, Bruchko."

The waiter brought us some coffee, thick and steaming hot. As Bobby stirred his, his smile turned into a frown. "We've been having more trouble with the land settlers. They've sent us several threatening letters."

The settlers had given us trouble before. Some were prison escapees who lived on the frontier to avoid arrest. They were interested in taking Motilone land for their own farms, and declaring the territory a refuge.

"What do they want now?" I asked.

"Oh, you know. More land. More of our land. They treat us like animals to be pushed in whatever direction is convenient for them."

"So you expect real trouble from them, or just threats?"

"I don't know, Bruchko. It may be real trouble. Most of the settlers seem to have sided with the outlaws, and that means they'll stop at very little. They are thinking that if the outlaws run us off our land they'll end up getting it, since the outlaws never will be able to own land themselves."

"So what are you going to do, Bobby?"

His face grew sad, and he looked down. "Well, I can tell you this much: we're not going to give up more of our land to them. We've given it up time after time, and there's just no end to it. This time we'll protect it ourselves. But, Bruchko," he said, looking up at me, "I hope, I pray that it won't come to that."

I had plenty of time to think about that as we rode the canoe up river. It was a seven-hour trip, and the big Briggs and Stratton motor made so much noise it was impossible to talk. It was incredible, unbelievable that the settlers were troubling us again. It was so two-faced. More than three thousand settlers had been treated by Motilone Indians in the Motilone health centers. They were happy to come to us when they needed help. The Motilones had given them their drugs and medical supplies free of charge. Yet, when they wanted Motilone land, the settlers would do anything to get it.

I looked back at Bobby, who was steering the boat, and smiled. How strange that I had gotten to this place, that I felt the way I did about these people. It was God who had brought me. I never would have come myself. And even if I had wanted to, I could never have made it past all the problems, past the loneliness, past the danger. In fact, I never would have left my home in Minneapolis if I had not had His powerful, determined Presence inside me.

As I sat in the canoe, I thanked God for Bobby, for the Motilones, for the jungle which was on all sides of us, even above us like a tent. Huge trees with slim trunks stretched high, looking for the sunlight that barely pierced to the jungle floor. Thick green moss hung on the sides of each tree, and beneath the trees were thick growths, head-high, of vines, bushes and ferns, all a brilliant green. When the river narrowed and we went in under the trees, it seemed as dark as night. The air was hot and humid, stifling. Bugs circled us and bit. But I was immensely happy. This was my home. Everywhere else I felt out of place.

We rode for five and a half hours. Neither of us tried to speak. Yet there was communication. We would point at some object and remember experiences we'd had. We saw no life on the river. A few bright birds would appear in the trees for a moment, then be gone. When we stopped the motor to refuel, we could hear animals calling. But there were no settlements, no signs of human life.

Suddenly we realized from the river bends that we were close to the communal home of Ayaboquina.

Bobby looked questioningly at me, and gestured in the direction of the home which was at the top of a bluff. *Do you want to stop?* he was asking. I nodded yes. He pulled in to the side of the river. We tied the canoe to a tree, then climbed the bluff quickly. Just at the top, a few feet from the home, was a large, new sign. It announced in bold letters that beyond was Motilone territory, and that settling it was illegal.

I gestured to the sign. "The government finally got it up, eh?"

"Yes. Two weeks ago."

We asked for Ayaboquina at the home, and one of the women told us that he was in the nearby clearing. They were building a new home, and there would be a school and health center nearby.

It was there that we had found Ayaboquina and had been threatened by Humberto Abril.

Later, I thought of those words, "For this cross I'll kill you." They were chilling, icy. Were they only a curse, only a threat? Or did they say more? Were they prophetic of something the cross was yet going to do to us?

It was for the cross that I could love the Motilones and be loved in return. But was it also for the cross that I would die? Was it also for the cross that Bobby would die?

2

Who is My God?

"Who is my God?" I asked. I was fourteen years old. "Who is He?"

There was no one to answer. Across the high school yard I could hear the thuds and whistles from a football practice. For the thousandth time I wished that I were good enough at sports to be asked to play.

But there was something besides sports on my mind . . . something that had been bothering me for days.

"Who is my God?" I asked myself again. "There's the Lutheran God whom we talk about in church. There's the God of all the Christian churches whom we study about in school. There's the God I've been reading about in the Bible. But which of them is *my* God?"

No answers came out of the frozen Minnesota sky. I began to walk home.

It didn't seem that anybody knew the answer. The Sunday before, I had gotten enough courage to ask my Sunday School teacher. He'd smiled a big bony smile. "Didn't you take your confirmation vows?"

I knew all about confirmation. While studying for it, I had learned theology. But I wanted to know God.

My dad would rather I didn't think about it. I hadn't asked him—but I knew what he would say. He'd look down at me with his crystal blue eyes and tell me that I was wasting both his time and mine.

Maybe I was. It didn't seem at all likely that there was any God other than the fierce Lutheran one. It frightened me just to think of Him.

This icy wind cutting my face is His wind, I thought. I kicked at the brown dead grass along the sidewalk. This morning it had been laced with snow. A few icy patches were left in the shadows of the gutters.

Why was I born? I'm too spindly . . . too nearsighted . . . too awkward. I can't even play football. When they throw a pass at me, it hits me, and they make fun of me.

I could see Kent Lange's freckled face ringed with dark, curly hair, his mouth stretched into a big laugh. He was my best friend. My stomach got a cold heaviness, like when I ate ice cream too fast.

Why did I take it all so seriously? It was only a game. *When I get home,* I thought, *I'll get out my books. Then all these problems will be forgotten.*

I loved to line up my books on my bed, to have them scattered around me in their different languages. For the last two nights I had been practicing my Greek by reading the Bible. I had a big leather Bible that was beautifully printed and bound, and I loved to leaf through the pages. For years I had been reading the Bible, mostly the Old Testament. Now that I was learning Greek, it was interesting to dip into the New Testament.

But for the time being, the Old Testament was still my favorite. I was enchanted by the histories, intrigued by the battles. Sometimes on Sunday afternoons I would read through many chapters at a time.

The prophets were different. They often frightened me so much that I would slam the Bible shut until I could convince myself that this was a "dream book," not actual prophecy. God's judgment was all too easy to imagine: the earth opening and people being carried down into the pit of eternal fire; Jesus coming with His armies of bright,

WHO IS MY GOD? / 21

fierce angels with swords to destroy all creation for its sinfulness.

It frightened me to think of God. Sometimes when I lost my temper I would realize what I was doing and would cringe inside, my stomach muscles tightening. Yet I couldn't stop, I would go ahead and fight, feeling terrible the whole time. Later I would think, *Oh God, I'm going to be judged.* I would be sorry, but would know inside that I would do the same thing again.

The New Testament seemed different. For two nights I had been reading the book of John. I was confused by it. Jesus didn't seem at all like He had been described to me. Or had I confused Jesus with the God I feared? Everywhere Jesus went people were changed by Him—and always for the better.

I thought of my Sunday School class. I knew every kid in it. I'd gone to church with them all my life. They'd never changed. None of us had ever changed.

Oh, there was lots of talk about change, all right. The minister told us, "You've got to change because God is going to damn the earth and its sinners. You must be holy, just as God is holy. That is what He demands of you. Short of His perfection is short of His eternity."

And that damnation frightened me. Sometimes Kent came to my house on Saturdays and we would talk about horror stories and movies we'd seen. We'd try to scare each other, and we'd giggle and stick our heads under the cushions. We enjoyed being scared. But sooner or later we would talk about God's judgment, about the burning pitch and the sky being rolled up like a scroll. Then we'd get very quiet. We knew that was no invention of a movie director or a story writer. It was real. It was going to come.

Mother was preparing dinner in the kitchen when I got home. I was chilled from the dry, bitter-cold wind. I took off my coat and hung it up, then went into the kitchen, rubbing my hands.

She pushed back one of her blond curls and looked at me. "How was school today, Bruce?"

"Fine," I said. "Where's Dave?"

She looked down. "Your brother and your dad had a fight. He's up in his room."

Suddenly I felt bone tired. Someone always was fighting in our house. Things seemed to go best when we didn't talk to each other.

I climbed the stairs to my room, noticing how each one was polished to a dark red—like a ripe cherry. I liked that. Everything should be in order. Everything should be neat and clean. Why couldn't our family be like that? To look at us you would think things were fine. My mother was a beautiful Swedish woman, perfect like a statue. None of my friends had a mother who looked like that. And my father was handsome, with a strong jaw and deep brown hair that was never out of place. But we seldom got along.

I went to my room and put my schoolbooks away. Then I got out my other books and put them on my bed. I had an English Bible, a Greek New Testament, and some books to help me understand the Greek.

I stretched my lanky body on the bed. My feet stuck over the edge. My books made a little circle around me. This was the closest thing to a home that I had. I felt comfortable here.

I read into the evening. My mother called me to dinner, and I went down to the silent ring of my family, still thinking about what I had been reading.

My father noticed that I wasn't saying anything.

"Why don't you contribute something to the rest of the family?" he asked. He spoke with great precision.

"I was just thinking about something else, Sir," I said.

"And what was that?"

I looked helplessly at my mother. I didn't want to have to talk.

"Bruce," my father said, "don't look at your mother. I'm the one speaking to you."

So I was forced to try to explain. I told him that I'd been reading the New Testament and that I didn't understand it very well.

"Of course you don't," he said. "It was written two thousand years ago. It's not expected to make sense today."

A mouthful of food stuck in my throat. I was tired of hearing my father dismiss things with a sentence. What did he know about it? I looked down at my plate. It was easier if we didn't talk at all.

As soon as I could be dismissed I went back to my room. Everything was wrong. I picked up my Bible, but the words swam around the page. My face felt hot.

I took off my glasses and lay down on the bed. "Stupid things," I said, looking at the thick lenses I had worn as long as I could remember. I hated them. Those glasses had gotten in my way in sports; had gotten me called four-eyes and bug-eyes for as long as I'd had them.

I put my head down. What was the point of getting mad at the glasses?

Surely *somewhere* there was someone who could help me. The apostle John had met Jesus and since then had never been the same. All the Gospels told about people being changed by Jesus. I longed for a change, too. But my God didn't care enough about me to do anything, I thought.

"Who is my God, anyway? Where is He?" I said to myself.

Maybe if I keep reading, I'll find the answer, I thought. But I didn't really expect to find something helpful. After all, the Bible was written before there were Lutherans. Then I came across a verse that shocked me, that sent electricity jingling through my body.

I sat up and read it again: "For the Son of man is come to seek and to save that which was lost." I knew God's justice, that He would judge me on the basis of my impurities— but here was a verse saying that Jesus had come to save the lost. I knew instantly who He was talking about. Me. But how was Jesus going to save me? And from what? Was He going to do some miracle?

A verse I had read in Romans began to make sense: "If thou shalt believe in thine heart that God hath raised him (Christ) from the dead, thou shalt be saved." And saved was the opposite from lost.

That's all? I thought. *Just believe? Shouldn't I have to do some great thing? Shouldn't I have to live a perfect life?* That was the idea I had gotten from my church.

I thought of all the things about myself that I didn't like. My temper. The bad thoughts that sometimes filled my mind. Could Jesus change these things?

Maybe He had been able to change water into wine two

thousand years ago. But what did that prove about Bruce Olson? I thought about all those people in the Gospels who were changed by Jesus. But what did they have to do with me?

Hours passed. There didn't seem to be any solution to my questions. I was tired. The clock on my dresser said it was two o'clock in the morning.

Then I felt, very suddenly and very strongly, that those questions weren't for me to answer.

I felt drawn to try to speak to Christ. Of course I had prayed before, only formally, in church, reading from the hymnal. This was different. I lay on my bed, face down, and spoke to Jesus. It was a simple talk, but it was the first I had ever really had with Him.

"Oh, Jesus," I said, "I've read about how everyone around You was changed. Now I want to be changed. I want peace and fulfillment like Paul and John and James and the other disciples. I want to be delivered from all my fears and . . ."

At that moment I felt a Presence in the room, like a stillness. I was at the same time small and quiet, huge and rearing, covering everything.

"Lord, I'm frightened by You," I continued. "You know I don't even like myself. Everything is messed up around me. And it's messed up in me, too. But please, God, I want to change. I can't do it myself. And I don't understand how You can do anything within me. But, Jesus, if You could change all those people in the Bible, I guess You can change me. Please, Jesus, let me know You. Make me new."

And then I knew that I was being saved. I felt miserable and broken, and sick of myself. But I also realized a peace coming into me. It wasn't something dead and passive, that peace. It wasn't just a silence ending the war inside me. It was alive, and it was making me alive. I could feel that I was going to be able to like myself. And I knew that I didn't ever want that peace, that stillness to go away.

I lay on my bed, feeling amazed, too astounded to move or even to think. I kept speaking to Jesus, knowing that He was there. Jesus was there. I didn't have to worry about the Lutheran God or the Christian God or anyone else's God. They weren't my problem. Jesus was my God my *personal* God. And I had just talked with Him.

3

Conflict

The peace was still there in the morning.

I've got to share this, I thought. *It will change my family completely. And the kids at church. They need to know Jesus, too.*

Sunday afternoons the Lutheran youth group met in the basement of the church. I arrived early. Only a few boys were there, standing in various parts of the room, talking.

I went over to a group of three whom I knew, and started explaining what had happened to me. I was smiling broadly, and expected them to react in the same way. Instead they got a careful, reserved expression on their faces.

Something was wrong, but I didn't know what. A few other boys came up and listened, all of them solemn. When I finished there wasn't a sound.

Then one of the boys looked up at the old wood ceiling and said, "So you've found a special door into heaven, eh Bruce?"

"Yeah, you've really gotten super-spiritual all of a sudden, Olson."

They didn't understand! I must not have explained it right.

"No, no that's not it at all," I said. "It's there for anyone, not just for me. I'm not trying to tell you I'm something special."

I looked back and forth across the little circle of cold, withdrawn faces. These were my peers! I wanted them to understand. But they were looking at me as though I were an animal in a zoo.

Pastor Peterson came up, and I turned to him. Here was someone who would understand. He could explain it better than I.

"What is it, boys?" he asked. "What's going on?" He turned to me. "What's happening, Bruce?"

He was a tall man with a thin red face. He had a huge Adam's apple that bobbed up and down distractingly when he talked.

I explained what I had been saying. He listened kindly, nodding as I talked. I felt relieved.

"Well, that's wonderful, that's fine, Bruce. I'm happy to hear that you've had such a fulfilling experience. But don't forget that you were confirmed in the Lutheran church, right here in this building, and at the moment of confirmation you dedicated yourself to Christ. The Christian life began for you even before that, however, when you were baptized and given your name."

"But when I took communion and had my confirmation, nothing of it was real to me," I said. "I was still the same." I remembered how I had walked home in my white confirmation robe, trying to feel somehow different, but saying to myself, *Is that all there is to it? I had hoped there was something more.*

Pastor Peterson's face, which had been friendly and warm, grew cold—like the boys' faces.

"Olson," he said, "I prayed over each of you boys when you were confirmed. Are you telling me that my prayers meant nothing? You've got to believe in your confirmation vows, that they were real and meaningful." His face grew a little redder. I wished that I had never brought the whole thing up. But I had to go on.

"Well, I believe in them now," I said. "Jesus is a reality to me now. I've been changed. I've begun to feel for people when I never did before." The words gushed out. I wanted them to stop, but they wouldn't. "Jesus is in my life now. If He was before, I never knew it."

Later, Pastor Peterson talked to me in private. He was stern. "Listen, Olson, you've gotten some kind of holy-roller ideas from somewhere. But don't give your life to fanaticism. Take the mask off. You're no different from anyone else."

I sat quietly, tired of trying to explain myself. How could something so good, so basically simple, make people so upset?

He leaned forward in his seat. "Bruce, when you come right down to it, Christianity is a moral imperative that obligates us to do right, to love our neighbors. That's the point of the whole thing."

After that, I really listened to his sermons. He preached about reform and about Christian ethics, but nowhere did he speak about the power for them. He spoke of change and gave a wonderful model of what we should be, but he didn't tell how we could begin to match up to the model.

I couldn't match up to the model either. I knew that. Not yet, anyway. But my life had changed, and it was changing more. I had peace with God. He was real, and I knew Him. My temper always had been a terrible problem. But after I came to know Jesus, it seemed to dissolve. Even my friends in the youth group, with all their jeering, didn't rub me the wrong way. I was frustrated and hurt, but only wanted them to have a personal encounter with Jesus, too.

My attitude toward school also changed. I began to be interested in what I was studying, because I could see how it related to Jesus. My mother began to enjoy going to PTA to see my improved grades.

I'd always liked languages, and I'd been studying Latin, Greek and Hebrew. Now I had a reason for studying them. In Greek and Hebrew I could read the Bible in its original languages, and in Latin I could read the writings of the early Christians.

But as school became more meaningful, church grew more painful. I would sweat through the services, wanting to shout back at Pastor Peterson that he didn't understand

Jesus. I stopped taking communion because I'd been taught that to take it you had to be in communion with other believers and God—and I didn't feel much communion with either the pastor or the congregation.

I had not told Kent Lange about my experience; in fact, I hadn't seen him very often since he had changed high schools. About two weeks after my encounter with Jesus, however, he came over on a Saturday afternoon. He'd run to the house and was breathing almost too hard to talk.

"Bruce, the most incredible thing has happened to me," he finally gasped out. "At church last night, I asked Jesus to come into my heart, like they tell you to do all the time, and Bruce, He did. I lost all track of what was going on in the service. Bruce, He was there, in the church, and in my heart, and I *knew* it."

I shut my eyes as a wave of relief and joy washed through me.

"Oh, Kent, that's great," I said. Then I told him about my own experience. We stood talking both at once. Then Kent jumped on me and we rolled around the room, wrestling, pushing each other, as we compared experiences.

"Kent, I just can't believe it. Both of us . . ." I was standing, looking at him. "But, Kent, what did you mean—that they always tell you to ask Jesus into your heart in church? They don't do that in my church. No one ever heard of it."

Kent told me about his church. It certainly sounded different from the dry Lutheran church I'd attended all my life. Nearly all of the people acknowledged Jesus as their Lord and Savior, Kent said.

The next day was Sunday, and Kent invited me to go to church with him. From the outside it was like any other church. But I felt excited. I'd never been to any non-Lutheran church.

Inside, it didn't look like a church to me. There were no pews, no elaborate altar decorations. It looked more like a school auditorium. Plenty of people already were there, but they weren't sitting in their seats. They were talking. It made me think of a hive of huge bees, buzzing about. In the Lutheran church everyone came in silently and immediately took his seat to pray.

We sat down in the folding chairs, toward the back.

When the service began, Kent's father, who was the minister, went to the front. "We're met together today to praise God for what He has done in our lives through His Son Jesus Christ," he said. "Let's all join in singing hymn number 38."

Everyone reached down and opened his hymnbook. It was a hymn I'd never heard before. Kent found the place, the piano began to play, the pipe organ roared, and the congregation sang. Somebody behind us began to clap his hands. Everyone else joined in. I was shocked. What was going on? Where was the reverence, the respect?

After the song, Mr. Lange returned to the podium. "Well, we're clapping in praise to the Lord," he said. "It's a beautiful song, and full of truth about what the Lord has done. And we're here in the house of the Lord today, and if you believe that God is real, say 'Amen.' " And everyone did—filling the hall with a big, booming sound. A—men!

But Mr. Lange put his hand to his ear and said, "Didn't anybody say 'Amen' out there? I couldn't hear it."

So they said it again, louder than ever. I squirmed. I thought everyone must be looking at me, the lone non-Amen-sayer. I remembered how once in the Lutheran church I had dropped my hymnal in the middle of the service and my mother had grabbed me and said, "Shhhh. Don't pick it up now. Stay standing up." And here were people saying "Amen" out loud.

A band was present that Sunday evening, and began to play. Everyone around me soon was tapping his foot.

Mr. Lange asked for "a testimony."

"God is with us this evening," he said. "We know that, because we're together reading His word and singing His praises. But we need a testimony. Who'll stand up and tell us what God has done for him."

I didn't expect anyone to be willing to do that. But before I knew it a man stood up and began telling about some of the problems his family had been having.

"But I praise God for those troubles," he said, "because He helped us with them. We were able to pray about them as a family, and He's really helping us solve our differences in love, day by day, and we're becoming closer as a family."

He had his whole family stand up. There were four boys

and some of them weren't too far from my age. The man reached out and hugged each of them. Then they hugged him and each other. They even hugged some of the people sitting near them. And everyone clapped.

It was all strange. But oh, how I wanted it. I wanted to be able to pray with my own family. I wanted to be hugged and accepted by my father!

Then came the sermon. It hadn't gone very far before the man sitting next to me leaned back and said, "Amen!" I nearly slid off my chair with surprise, it was so close and so unexpected.

But even though it was strange, I was attracted to it. Here was a church where people seemed to know the reality of Christ.

I went back to the Wednesday night service. Then I went to the Thursday night prayer service, and again to an evening service on Friday. Then all day Sunday. I couldn't get enough of it. And I was learning much from the Scriptures. I had been reading the Bible, of course, but Mr. Lange's messages opened my eyes to things I'd never thought or dreamed of.

I suppose I knew there would be trouble with my parents. It wasn't long in coming. They had been upset when I first told them about the reality of Christ in my life. My father was particularly apprehensive about this. If it couldn't be explained in Lutheran terms it wasn't understandable—or acceptable. He had been confirmed a Lutheran, and to him being a Lutheran meant respectability. He thought that I was trying to be better than he when I started telling about finding Christ.

He tried to talk me out of going to the interdenominational church. When I came home he would look up from the paper and say, "Well, here's our holy-roller son back from the kingdom of God. What's the message of God to us poor sinners tonight?"

He said that every night—every single night that I came home from church. It got so that I couldn't stand it. I would run by him and up to my room and bury my head in the pillow, trying to stop the ringing of his voice in my head.

He also would clap his hands in imitation of the church (because I had at first tried to describe it to them) and sing,

"Oh yes, Jesus, we're going to be saved. Oh yes, Jesus, come down on us tonight."

It was five miles to the interdenominational church, and I had no way to get there, other than walking. I would go to the Lutheran church each Sunday morning to appease my mother, and then I'd set out for the other church. It was winter, and the wind would blow up my pant legs and the sleeves of my coat. The cold would come up through the soles of my shoes from the ice-covered sidewalks, go through my feet and climb up my legs. There were days when every second of the walk was agonizing.

Then I would reach the church. Inside it was warm. Friendly faces would look up and greet me. We would open the Bible and my body would sink down into itself and relax, like a cat preparing to sleep. But my mind would be wide awake. I found constant happiness when I was reading His Word.

When church was over, I would linger as long as I could. I always refused a ride from anyone. I was too proud—or too shy.

My father had done everything but command me to stop attending the church. One night I started for home late. On the way I had to cross Lake Street Bridge. The wind, with nothing to block it, swept waves of powdery snow across the roadway and into my face. I also could hear it whistling underneath, down by the frozen water. I wanted to rest, but I was afraid to stop. I remembered stories of trappers freezing to death because they had stopped to rest and couldn't get up again.

Across the bridge I could see the lights of the houses, beautiful homes like white shells in the snow.

"Oh, Jesus," I whispered, "help me."

But I went on and somehow walked up the incline, past the houses to my own house. It was dark. I felt relieved to be home. I reached for the doorknob, and had trouble gripping it. My ice-coated mitten slipped off the cold brass.

I went through the slow procedure of taking off my mitten. I finally had to work it off with my teeth, my fingers were just too stiff. I put my hand on the doorknob again, and turned it.

The door was locked.

I tried it again to be sure. There was no question. My parents had forgotten that I was out.

I hated to wake them up, but I had to get in, so I rang the doorbell. I watched the window of their bedroom, waiting for the light to go on. It didn't. I rang the doorbell again. No response.

My mother could sleep through that noise, but my father was too light a sleeper. I knew he was awake. I called to him.

"Dad, it's me, Bruce. Come down and open the door for me, please. I'm freezing."

There was no reply. Although I didn't want to, I started to cry, the tears freezing on my face.

"Dad, please. It's Bruce. Please let me in."

I took a deep breath and held it in. Then I felt a little more calm. I looked up at the dark window again. It seemed to be looking back at me, like a dark, hooded eye. Finally I thought of the Langes. I knew they would take me in. But it was two miles to their house, back along the way I had come.

"Please, Dad," I called, and waited. There was no response. I turned on my heel and began to run. I ran as hard as I could until I couldn't run any farther. When I stopped, I was already across the bridge. My breath was heaving, and the cold air burned my lungs each time I breathed.

I made it to the Langes, exhausted and shaking. They got up and gave me a warm place to sleep.

That was the worst time. But it wasn't the last. I never knew whether I would find the house locked or unlocked when I got home.

My mother was caught in the middle. She feared my father, but there was little she could do to constrain him. I remember coming home one afternoon and finding her in the kitchen, leaning against the stove with tears staining her beautiful, flawless face and dripping down in splashes on the burners.

It frightened me.

"Mom, what's the matter?" I asked.

Her voice shook. She started talking twice and couldn't.

Finally she said, "Bruce, what's going to hold our family together?"

I thought I knew the answer. I had been trying to give it all along. But now, when I was asked, it seemed difficult to phrase.

"Mom, we need to be real Christians. With Jesus in our lives, there is hope for us," I said.

I hadn't expected to make her angry. But when she looked at me, I knew she was both angry and hurt—not only at me, but at life.

"Oh, Bruce," she said. "How can you say that when it's your Jesus who is the source of half our problems? At least before Him we could all tolerate each other. But He's stirred up everything."

It was true. But I didn't know then that Christ had said He would bring divisions as well as unity to people.

I was discovering that the cross of Christ meant more than joy and peace. It meant suffering, too—suffering that was necessary to bring a later hope.

But there would be plenty of opportunity for me to learn that lesson.

4

A Missionary?

When I was sixteen, the interdenominational church I now attended regularly held a missionary conference. It was something new to me, and I was intrigued. Missionaries from all over the world gathered to talk about the areas in which they were working. For the first time I heard the term "Great Commission." It had a mysterious ring to it.

One of the missionaries, Mr. Rayburn, "served" in New Guinea. He was a short, dumpy man with an expression of continual surprise. The night he spoke he wore a bright green polka-dot shirt, black pants, and dirty tennis shoes. I was surprised that anyone would dress that sloppily to speak in church, but I soon discovered that he had a forceful message.

The church was full. I had been reading about New Guinea, and was looking forward to a first-hand report.

Mr. Rayburn showed movies that he had taken. In one scene, a man was eating a rat. You could just see the tail of the rat hanging out of the man's mouth—then, phht, it was gone.

"That fellow eating the rat there. He's not a Christian," Mr. Rayburn said.

Poor fellow, I thought, remembering how miserable I had been before becoming a Christian.

There were other pictures: some of extreme poverty in the midst of modern cities, some of "natives" and their odd clothes, houses, and eating habits. Then Mr. Rayburn made his appeal.

"These people are starving, dying of disease, living in ignorance, eating rats. But most of all they are starving for the knowledge of Jesus Christ. They are dying *lost,* without knowing how Jesus Christ can save them from their sins. Can you sit comfortably in your seats and accept that? Do you care about these men and women, living in squalor and filth? They're dying, damned to eternal condemnation! And what do you do? Maybe if you're really virtuous you put a little money in the collection plate on Sunday morning. Maybe you put in a dollar to reach these people starving for the Gospel.

"But Jesus wants more of you. He wants more than your lip service to the great cause of missions. It's your responsibility to take the Gospel of Christ to these people. Otherwise their blood will be required of you."

That night I had nightmares. I dreamt that the man eating the rat pulled the rat's tail back out of his mouth. It became a whip, and he used it to beat me while he screamed, "My blood is required of you. My blood is required of you."

I woke up in a cold sweat.

That can't be right, I thought. *God's not like that. He's a God of love. He loves me.*

"But do you love Him?" the question came.

"Yes, I love Him. Of course I love Him. How could I not?"

"Won't you serve Him, then?"

"Serve Him? I am serving Him. I study the Word. I've shared with all my friends what He means to me. Isn't that serving Him?"

The next evening I talked with Mr. Rayburn. "You're wasting your time here," he said. "The whole world is damned, and it's your responsibility to give them the truth."

For weeks after the conference I quarreled with God.

"But why are You set on making me a missionary?" I asked. "Why can't I be Your servant here in Minneapolis?"

My aim was to become a professor of languages, to get a Ph.D. in philology. But something within me said, "That isn't what God wants you to do."

"Listen, God, these missionaries are ridiculous," I argued. "They wear tennis shoes in the pulpit. Their prayer letters aren't even written in decent English. And their theology. They're always talking about hell and damnation. Where is their love for the people they're living among? They're failures, Lord. They can't make it in normal life, so they go off to be missionaries.

"But I can succeed here, Father. Everyone agrees. Why should I have to work with naked, starving people?"

God never told me why. But He did change my heart. Gradually my pleasant sane dream of becoming a linguistic professor vanished into this ridiculous idea of going to other countries to talk to savages about God. I knew it wouldn't make sense to my parents; it didn't even make much sense to me. But over the months, as I walked to school, as I sat and daydreamed in class, as I read the Bible, He gave me something I'd never bargained for: compassion.

I couldn't fight it. God made no demands. He didn't force me. But I found myself irresistibly interested in other countries, in other cultures. As I continued to read, South America captured my attention, and I began to identify with the people there. Soon I found myself dreaming of this enchanting land and her people. I gave in to God.

I told Kent Lange that I had been "called" to be a missionary to South America.

"You? *You?* A missionary?" Kent's face broke into a grin. "Bruce, that's impossible. Don't you remember when we were Boy Scouts—what a great adventurer you were then?"

I grinned with him. My parents would drop me off at the front door of the Methodist Church where the Boy Scout troop met. I would go through the church and out the back, over to King's Pharmacy where I would buy a book and read it until it was time to go home. The great outdoors had never interested me.

Nominal friends also discouraged me. They reminded me of my physical disabilities: I'd had bronchitis when I was younger, and I still wasn't too strong.

"And Bruce," they told me, "you've got a great life ahead of you as a linguist. Don't throw your abilities away."

It was a convincing argument. However, I was changing my mind about the stature of missionaries. When I'd looked into mission board requirements, I'd discovered to my surprise that you needed a Bible institute education (or its college equivalent) to be accepted. So I postponed my decision and went away to Penn State in the fall of 1959. For either vocation—linguistic professor or missionary—I would need a college education.

But I couldn't escape from my fascination with the people of South America. I compulsively read books on their history and culture, and became especially interested in two countries: Colombia and Venezuela.

I enjoyed my classes at Penn State, and did well. But I was lonely. I made few friends. And nagging at the back of my mind was the thought that I should be planning to go to either Colombia or Venezuela in the near future.

I transferred to the University of Minnesota the next year. I had hoped that by being home again our family situation would improve. But it was no better. I had been praying that God would change both my parents' attitude toward me and my attitude toward them. I knew I wasn't of much help to them. But my father in particular remained rigid, and it was too much of a strain for me. We alternated between coldly ignoring each other and openly arguing. Somehow I was never quite an adult in their eyes.

Through it all, my compassion for the people of South America continued to grow. What had been a lukewarm commitment became a driving urge. Finally one evening I decided that I wouldn't wait until I finished school. I would visit South America now. Maybe I would find peace in my heart when I got there.

I began the process of applying to a well-known mission board in Venezuela. It was a tedious, slow process, and I felt school chafing against me. Once I had made the decision to leave the U.S., it didn't make sense to me to keep going to school. And the thought of going to Venezuela was becoming more and more exciting.

I had an inner peace about it, too. I knew that, irrational as it seemed, I was doing the right thing. I was obeying God.

Then one day I received my long-awaited reply from the mission board. With great excitement I opened the envelope. I found a single sheet.

"Dear Mr. Olson: We are sorry to inform you that we cannot accept you at this time for missionary service. You understand, I trust, that . . . "

I didn't finish the letter. I couldn't. The words seemed to have lost all their meaning—as though they were written in hieroglyphics. I stared at it. My mother came into the room and noticed that something was wrong.

"What's the matter, Bruce?" she asked, putting a hand up to my forehead, checking to see if I had a fever.

I closed my eyes and breathed a deep sigh. "It's nothing, Mom," I said. "Just some bad news."

She looked questioningly at me, but I couldn't explain. Not then, anyway. I turned and left the room.

Later when I was over the original shock, I felt better. *Well, at least that's over and done with,* I thought. *I won't have to worry about God wanting me in South America for awhile at least.*

And for a few days I felt relieved. I enrolled in new classes at the University of Minnesota and really looked forward to studying. My dream of becoming a professor of languages returned. I could pick up where I had left off, and forget South America like a nightmare is forgotten after waking.

But many times as I studied in the library I felt God nudging me. "Bruce, I want you in South America."

"But, Lord, I tried that. Don't You remember? I was turned down."

"Turned down by whom?"

"Why, by the mission board, of course."

It was as though God were smiling at me, amused and tolerant. "Bruce, I didn't turn you down. I want you in South America. Follow me."

"God, this is ridiculous. How can I go down there without

a mission board? You want me to go down there without anyone to take care of me? I mean—without protocol and all?"

"Bruce, I'm in South America too."

And then slowly, unwillingly, I began to see what God had been trying to teach me. He hadn't called me, really, to be a missionary like Mr. Rayburn. He had called me to Himself, to be like His Son, Jesus Christ. And He wanted me to follow Him to South America. Now.

I knew my parents would never be able to accept it. Even the thought of going with a well-established mission board had upset them. To go all by myself . . . they would consider that impossible.

So I went to Chicago on the train to get my passport and visa without telling my parents. I had only enough money for the round-trip train ticket: nothing for food or a place to sleep. All the way there I prayed that God would take care of what I needed.

I was hungry when I arrived in Chicago. I had about thirty cents in my pocket. I found my way out of the huge, bustling, echoing station and onto the sidewalk. I stopped for a moment to get my bearing. It was hot and windy. I glanced down and saw some green out of the corner of my eye. It looked like money.

I picked it up and unfolded it. It was a ten-dollar bill!

"Wow. Thank you, God," I whispered. I looked around expecting someone to claim it. No one was near. There was no way of finding who had dropped it. I could keep it.

Later, a friend gave me the name and address of a missionary in Venezuela. I wrote him and asked if he would be willing to meet me at the airport. I told him that I was a student, and that I was interested in missions. He wrote back, telling me enthusiastically that he'd be sure to be at the airport, and that he'd show me around Caracas and help me find a place to stay. That helped calm my mother's fears.

I showed both of my parents pictures of Caracas, and told them about its high standard of living and highly-civilized Western culture. But nothing would convince them. They were sure that any place other than the U.S. or Europe was barbaric, and that I was throwing my life away.

But they let me go. I was given enough money for my plane ticket to Caracas, and seventy dollars for expenses. I hoped it would be enough.

I barely made my plane. I had dropped my ticket at a big church send-off, and someone had found it and reported it just in time. When I got it, there were only a few minutes left for a quick good-bye to my parents and to the Langes. Then I went up the loading ramp and boarded the plane. The stewardess showed me to my seat, and I sat down and tried to relax.

For a moment, panic flooded me. What on earth was I doing? I was nineteen years old. I had seventy dollars, no knowledge of Spanish, no concrete plans. Only a drive within from God that nearly everyone else thought was foolish.

At least Mr. Saunders, the missionary to whom I'd written, would be at the airport to meet me.

I settled back in my seat and watched as the airplane left the ground behind. The checkered fields and the trees gradually became a single green blur—then were lost to my sight as the plane was enveloped in clouds.

5

First Meeting with Indians

A small boy sat next to me on the plane. He looked at me
with curiosity.

"Hello," I said.

He opened his mouth and a long stream of Spanish came
out.

I laughed and put up my hands. *"No comprendo."*

He stopped talking and looked puzzled.

"Americano," I said, pointing to myself. I picked up the
newspaper, printed in Spanish, which the stewardess had
given me, and tried to read a sentence out loud. The boy
showed no signs of understanding, but I didn't let that stop
me. Suddenly he said, *"Bien, bien,"* and I knew I'd pro-
nounced something correctly. But I had no idea what it meant.

I had to laugh at myself. Here I had studied Greek, Hebrew,
and Sanskrit, yet had never studied Spanish. *Sometimes,* I
thought, *God is not very practical.*

As the hours went by, I got more and more nervous.
Finally Venezuela came into sight.

43

I pressed against the window to watch the plane land. As we got lower I could see the mountains rising far behind the coastline. After circling over the ocean, the plane touched down at a modern airport on the coast.

When I stepped out of the plane, the Venezuelan heat rushed over me. It was incredible. By the time I had walked to the terminal I was sweating profusely.

As I stood in line to go through customs, I looked around anxiously for Mr. Saunders. The glass partitions gave me a clear view of waiting family members and I breathed a sigh of relief as I spotted a familiar figure. But after my two hours in the customs section, I discovered I was mistaken.

No one was waiting for a nineteen-year-old from the United States.

I got my luggage and sat on it, expecting Mr. Saunders to come around the corner at any minute. Every time I heard footsteps I looked up, ready to greet him, then sank back when I saw it was a janitor or a Venezuelan businessman.

I couldn't believe Mr. Saunders had forgotten me. Something must have delayed him.

But no one came. Then I was alone except for a janitor who was mopping the floor. I didn't know what to do. I was afraid that if I left, Mr. Saunders would come and I would miss him. I felt foolish sitting in the empty room waiting for him. I wished I was home.

Finally I carried my luggage to the ticket counter, and asked if someone had been looking for a Mr. Olson. The ticket man listened intently, then repeated probably the only English phrases he knew. "I'm sorry. I don't speak English." He went back to his work.

I looked around the room. "Anyone here speak English?" I asked loudly. No one turned.

Then a priest walked in, an elderly man in flowing black robes. I rushed over to him and tugged on his sleeve until he came with me to the ticket counter. There I spoke to him in Latin—and he understood! What a wonderful feeling to be understood!

The priest was in a hurry, though. He translated my questions to the man at the ticket counter—who didn't know a thing about a Bruce Olson or a Mr. Saunders. Before I could ask any more questions, the priest was off again.

What was I going to do? What could I do, except wait? He *had* to come.

But he didn't. At one o'clock in the morning, when I was the only person still at the terminal, a Pan Am attendant walked over to me. In English he told me that I would have to leave. No more flights were expected until morning, and I couldn't stay in the airport overnight.

I ended up in a luxurious hotel in the vicinity, but all I could think of was how much it cost me. My seventy dollars would be gone in a week!

The next day I got up early and walked around the hotel grounds, trying to decide what to do. The sun was bright and it already was hot. To conserve money, I went without breakfast and lunch. But when five o'clock came, I was too hungry to resist.

I had no way of contacting Mr. Saunders except by mail, and by the time I got a letter to him I would be completely broke. I couldn't ask for advice because I didn't know Spanish.

Then a strange thing happened. The next morning a young man stopped me and asked if I was an American. He was a cheerful looking fellow with snappy black eyes. Speaking very poor English, he introduced himself as Julio, and told me that he was a college student at the University of Caracas.

"What are you doing here in Venezuela?" Julio asked.

"I want to work with the Indians," I said. "I expected to be met by one of the missionaries who works in the Orinoco, but something went wrong. He never showed up."

Julio frowned. "You're not staying there, are you?" He pointed at the hotel.

I shrugged. "Where else? I don't know Caracas."

"Well, you won't get to know it staying at that place. Why it's just for . . . for . . . "

I laughed. "It's for Americans, you were going to say? Well, I'm an American."

"Okay," he said, "you're an American." He smiled. "Too bad for you. But you shouldn't stay there. Why don't you come home with me? We'll put you up. My family will be glad to have you."

My heart jumped. In no time we were lugging my suitcases onto a bus that took us up the beautiful mountains to Caracas—which Julio told me was the most modern city in South America. But I was shocked to see the thousands of squatters' huts on the mountainside, made of cardboard boxes and plywood crates.

When we arrived at Julio's house, he introduced me to his mother, a pleasant, heavy-set woman. She spoke no English, but with her gestures she let me know I was welcome. A stream of Julio's brothers and sisters trailed after her.

I was given a small room upstairs with one window permanently nailed shut, and one bare light bulb. But I was happy to have a place to stay, and they soon made me the center of their attention. I asked Julio and his brothers and sisters the Spanish names of different things, and began to learn the language. I also was introduced to Colombian food, and loved it.

But in a few days, I began to feel restless. I had difficulty communicating with anyone when Julio was gone, and I had nothing to occupy my time. I wanted to help this family in some way, but couldn't figure out how to do it. I often wandered through the streets of Caracas, wishing I could talk with people. I felt uneasy about sharing Julio's family's food and house: they obviously weren't prepared financially to have another family member. Also I began to feel in the way.

One day when Julio came home he asked, "Are you serious about wanting to live with the Indians?" We had talked about it before. To him, the Indians were just curiosities from whom to collect artifacts for rustic decor.

"Yes, I am," I said.

"Well, then there's a fellow you had better meet. He's a medical doctor who lives near the Orinoco River. He's employed by the government's Indian Commission. Furthermore, he's an American. His wife is a friend of a friend of our family."

I followed him down the street until we came to a small cafe. There Julio introduced me to Dr. Christian. A tall, slender man of about forty, he was sitting in a little cane chair, his long legs stretched out, holding a drink and smoking a cigaret.

"So you're interested in Indians," he said. "What for?"

I hesitated a moment, wanting to phrase my answer just right. "I just want to have the opportunity of meeting them and seeing their way of life. Maybe later I can be of some help to them."

He smiled, leaning forward a little. "What makes you think you can help them? Do you have any skills they need?"

When I didn't answer immediately, he held up his drink and stared at it. "You wouldn't even like the Indians," he said. "They're dirty and ignorant. There's nothing noble about them, except that they care for their own, even if they ask others to do it."

"What are you working with them for, then?" I countered.

He laughed. "Good question." He shrugged. "It's a job. I have to do something with my medicine. This is as interesting as anything—and it involves travel."

There was a short silence. Julio left.

"What Indians do you work with?" I asked.

"Oh, several tribes on the Orinoco River." He began to tell me about them, and as he did his attitude changed. Little crinkly laugh lines appeared around the corners of his mouth. He really loved the Indians, and it was fascinating to listen to him.

Then he stopped talking, and studied me. "All right," he said, "if you're serious about this you can come with me. I'm going next week, and I'll be gone for a month and a half."

I kept a calm exterior, but my heart raced. We shook hands and talked about arrangements. Then I left. As soon as I had put a block between myself and the cafe I let out a big whoop and ran down the street, dodging people on the sidewalk!

A week later we were in Puerto Ayacucho loading staples, supplies and drugs onto a truck that would take them—and us—to transport canoes on the High Orinoco—a sixty kilometer trip on their only out-of-town road. People were crowding onto the truck, shouting back and forth. A big, lumbering DC-3 had carried us into the little town that morning.

As we finished lashing down the cargo, people were hanging off the truck on all sides. We climbed up onto the top of the truck with them. A big jug of wine was passed over to us;

I passed it along to the man next to me. Everyone was talking. The truck started up and lumbered ahead onto the thin strip of dirt road. We entered the trees and immediately the town was out of sight. Ahead was savanna, interspersed with spots of jungle.

When we reached Samariapo we were sore and tired. The constant jolting of the truck had exhausted us. This was the end of the road. From Samariapo we would have to travel into the high Orinoco by boat.

We unloaded our cargo and took it down to the muddy, yellow Orinoco where Dr. Christian had two huge dugout canoes bound together. We filled them with our supplies for the next month, and then, with two guides to navigate day and night, we set out upriver.

It took us more than a week to reach the first Indian settlement. Mile after mile of the river rolled behind us. I soon lost track of the bends—and of the deadly wooden snouts sticking out of the water.

The rich vegetation on either side of the banks was unchanging. Occasionally we would reach a small clearing where a settler had his shack. Always he—or someone in his family—would look up from his work or run to the river bank to watch us. But for the most part, we saw no sign that men had ever been up the river before.

"Most settlers are farther up the Orinoco inlets where the lands are less apt to flood," Dr. Christian explained. I was excited, and asked endless questions about the Indians and about the missionary work there. I hoped to meet some of the missionaries, including Mr. Saunders, for this was the area in which he worked. I was sure he'd be friendly and apologize for forgetting to meet me at the airport.

At one point, Dr. Christian looked over at me. "You'll never fit in with these missionaries," he said. "They're a mess."

"What do you mean?"

He waved his hand. "You'll see."

We finally reached the first Indian village on the high Orinoco. From the riverbank I could see a small group of round huts. There were no Indians in sight. I felt somewhat apprehensive, but Dr. Christian routinely tied the canoes to a tree on the bank, and we stepped out.

All around us was the disgusting smell of human excrement and, as we walked up to the village, I could see flies buzzing around piles of filth only a few feet from the peoples' huts.

Dr. Christian didn't seem at all perturbed. A few of the natives greeted us, and he talked with them, having learned some of their vocabulary on a previous visit. Most of the Indians, however, had been frightened when they heard our canoes and had hid in the jungle.

One by one they came out of hiding, and Dr. Christian examined those who had ailments, gave them shots or pills, and made suggestions about sanitation. Their eyes glowed when he spoke in their language, and Dr. Christian obviously enjoyed their company. He treated each one patiently, trying to explain everything as well as he could.

We stayed there only for the day, then continued up the Orinoco to the point where the Mavaca River junctures into the Orinoco.

"You'll have to live with the Indians before you can begin to understand what their life is like," Dr. Christian said.

As I thought about it, a little chill went through me, but I decided I could be left for three weeks at the Mavaca while Dr. Christian continued upriver and into the other tributaries. He could pick me up again on his way back. I was particularly interested in staying at that particular place because Mr. Saunders worked near it. My meeting with him, however, was a great disappointment.

"What makes you think you can come down to South America without a mission agency?" he asked right after we had been introduced. "You just want to come down and impose on us. You think we'll have to take care of you. But you're wrong. You're on your own, Buster." He turned and walked off.

I was at the mission compound only a short time. The various missionaries there were extremely guarded in their approach to me. They did tell me that they were having "a certain amount of success at reaching the Indians with the Gospel of Jesus Christ," but that now there was "a great deal of persecution of the Christians by the other Indians." They had been cut off from the rest of the tribe.

Since the missionaries offered me no accommodations,

Dr. Christian dropped me off on the north part of the Mavaca River with a group of Indians whom the missionaries said weren't Christians. They spoke a broken Spanish. I had learned to speak it a little by that time, so we had a crippled communication—much better than my first encounter at the international airport in Venezuela.

I couldn't believe that these were the Indians the missionaries had described. These Indians persecute anyone? Impossible. They were too innocent. They allowed me to accompany them when they went hunting, and when I couldn't keep up their pace, someone stayed behind with me. When I tripped over vines and roots, they helped me up. They shared everything that they owned. I ate their food, slept in their hammocks. How could these Indians be "persecutors"?

When Sunday came I suggested to one of them that we all go to the church which wasn't far from their camp, and listen to stories about God. He looked at me and frowned. "No, we don't do that."

"Why not?"

"Those Christians, they're strange."

He wouldn't say more, but he did take me to the chief of the village, a big, strong character who laughed when he was told what I wanted to know.

"Listen," he said, "those Christians don't care about us any more. Why should we care about them?"

"How do you know that they don't care about you? They're of your tribe."

"Why, they've rejected everything about us," he said. "They won't sing our songs now. They sing those weird, wailing songs that are all out of tune and don't make sense. And the construction which they call a church! Have you seen their church? It's square! How can God be in a square church? Round is perfect." He pointed to the wall of the hut in which we sat. "It has no ending, like God. But the Christians, their God has points all over, bristling at us. And how those Christians dress! Such foolish clothes . . ."

I thought of the Indian Christians I had seen at the missionary compound. They had been taught how to dress in clothes with buttons, how to wear shoes, how to sing Western songs.

Is that what Jesus taught, I asked myself. *Is that what Christianity is all about? What does the good news of Jesus Christ have to do with North American culture?* In Bible times there was no North American culture. Were the missionaries making a mistake in their preaching? Of course, it probably made them happy to see the Indians dressed like Americans, singing "Rock of Ages." But was that the only way Jesus could be worshipped? And was there a certain amount of satisfaction in having the Indian Christians persecuted by the rest of the tribe? I began to wonder.

I decided to try to tell the Indians what the Gospel really was about, but it was difficult. Not only was my Spanish poor, but I had to overcome their suspicion and mistrust of "foreign missionaries." The Indians would listen politely to my explanations, then point in the general direction of the Indian Christians and shake their heads.

"We don't want to become like them" they would say emphatically. "Our way is right."

6

Last-Minute Help

After three weeks, Dr. Christian returned and we went back to Puerto Ayachucho where he kept a suite of rooms in a hotel. He invited me to stay there while he went on to Caracas.

Once again I was alone. My money was gone. The suite of rooms, crammed with the vases and china figurines Mrs. Christian liked to collect, felt small. I also was uncomfortable staying in someone else's private home and wished that I was back in the Orinoco jungle.

However, Puerto Ayachucho was a pleasant frontier town so I went out early each day to walk. The streets, shaded by almond trees planted in the sidewalks, were never crowded so I was free to pray and think.

The mission board with which Mr. Saunders was associated, had a large house in town. One day I met Bob, one of the missionary kids. He was eighteen, sandy-haired, with a big, boyish smile. Because he was only a year younger than I, we soon were having a good time. It was a pleasure to be able to speak English after straining at Spanish for several months. We compared stories and told jokes. Later that day another missionary kid named Tom joined us. He was a little older, but had a good sense of humor, and kept us all laughing.

When it began to get late, Tom said, "Bob and I have to be back in time for dinner." He could see that I hated to see them go. "Look," he added, "I wish you could come for dinner, but my dad, well . . . he wouldn't."

"Oh," I said. It was the same thing the other missionaries had told me. If they offered me hospitality, they thought it would commit them to taking care of me.

I went back to the dark and empty apartment, sat down on the sofa and put my hands behind my head. In doing so, I knocked a ceramic vase off the shelf. It broke with a crash. Trembling, I swept up the pieces and threw them away.

How I ached to get out of that apartment, to be with friends. But where could I go?

I lay down on my bed. "Oh, Lord," I prayed. "I don't have anything. No money . . . no friends. Christians here won't accept me. I'm not a missionary with a home board, so I have no support either from there or here. Please help me. Please keep me sane."

The next day there was no sign of Tom or Bob on the street. I decided to call on them at the mission station. When I knocked at the door, it opened just a crack.

"What do you want?" a voice asked.

"I'd like to see Tom, if I may," I replied.

Tom came to the door, obviously embarrassed. "I'm sorry, I'm not allowed to see you any more," he said.

"Why not?"

"My father says that you've been put out of fellowship. That means none of the missionaries are supposed to greet you."

"Out of fellowship? Why?" I knew my voice was rising, but I couldn't stop it.

Tom shrugged. "You won't obey them. They told you to go back to the States, join the mission, then come here and work."

"How could I even get back? Will they buy my ticket? And since when do I have to obey their orders?" My breath was coming fast.

Tom squirmed; hesitated. "I don't think I should talk to you about this any longer," he said. "Good-bye." He shut the door.

I walked down to the city square, feeling more lonely than ever. I wanted to run. But to where?

I sat on a bench in the square, wishing I could stay there in the sun forever.

After an hour or more, a priest approached and started a conversation. He said he was an Italian, and was teaching English to high school students, but dreaming of working with the Indians. He had never been able to go upriver to see the settlements. When I told him of my experience with Dr. Christian, he was fascinated. In spite of my prejudice against Catholics—especially against the clergy—I soon was happily engaged in conversation, and forgot my troubles. And when he got up and left to teach his class, I continued to sit in the sun, feeling somewhat cheered.

A little later a group of boys came up the walk, grinning at me self-consciously. They surrounded me, and took turns shaking my hand and saying, "Hello" with an exaggerated accent that made it sound like "Hey-loe." After that ceremony, one stepped forward, looked up at the sky and recited, "We wish for to invite you to our school class to talk of English."

Trying not to laugh, I thanked him solemnly, then followed them to their school where, not too surprisingly, the priest was the teacher. I spent at least an hour there, talking about America.

After school the boys crowded around me. One of them went to get his older brother, a university student home on Christmas break. I was introduced to him. He was short and muscular, with heavy dark eyebrows and bronze skin. He had a fierce look, but his mannerisms were gentle. His name was Rafael. He invited me to stay with his family, and I accepted. I discovered later that it was unthinkable among responsible Latin families to let a young person such as myself be alone. I also discovered that they believed when you do good to others, someone will care for your children when they are away from home. But at the time, I wasn't worried about the reasons. I just was glad to be accepted at last.

Rafael's house, in the poorest district of town, consisted of one room. It had a dirt floor, dark walls and a thatched roof. Cockroaches were everywhere. I slept in a hammock, as did the rest of the family. But I couldn't have cared less.

The next morning Rafael woke me while it was still dark. "Hurry," he said, "it's the first day of the Christmas celebration." We joined crowds of people in the streets. It was fun. We ran up and down, shooting off firecrackers and cherry bombs in the cool, early-morning air, jostling against other happy people and talking and yelling at each other. It was like the Fourth of July in Minnesota.

At five o'clock all the people started moving toward the church.

"Come on, let's go to mass," Rafael said.

I shook my head. "I can't. I'm a Protestant."

He pulled my arm. "It doesn't matter. Come along."

I looked at him. He was now my friend. How could I refuse to go to mass with my friend? This was a big event for him and his family. So I went along.

Those were wild days. Every morning we got up early, threw firecrackers, then went to mass, and I thoroughly enjoyed it.

But when the missionaries heard that I was attending mass, they completely cut me off. Since they'd already said I was out of fellowship, however, I couldn't see that it made too much difference, although their words of condemnation hurt.

Nothing would please them anyway, I decided, *except my leaving—and I'm not about to do that—not now.*

At last I could comprehend a little of what God was trying to teach me. So what if the missionaries had rejected me! So what if the poeple I had counted on most didn't act the way I thought they should. Jesus had not rejected me. He had led me to the Venezuelan nationals.

It was His plan I was following, and He would use every experience for my good.

After Christmas, Rafael had to make a trip, then go back to the University at Caracas. I didn't want to stay in his house while he was gone, so I made plans to leave when he did.

"But where are you going?" he asked.

I told him that I was going to Caracas, too; that Dr. Christian had described an American-Venezuelan cultural exchange program there that I might be able to get involved in.

"But where will you stay?" Rafael asked. "You can't just go to Caracas and walk around. Riots are going on, and there's lots of anti-American feeling."

He gave me the address of the private boarding house he stayed in, and a letter of presentation to the owners.

"This is the best place in all of Caracas," he said. "It's cheap, and clean, and in old Caracas. We all stay there."

What I didn't tell Rafael was that I had no way to get to Caracas. Yet I knew, somehow, that it would work out. I made plane reservations.

The day I was to leave, I stood by my suitcases in Rafael's house, wondering what I should do. I had already said goodbye to all my new friends. But Caracas was a long way off for a penniless young American.

Then Rafael's little brother came in with a letter for me—the first letter I'd received since I had left Caracas with Dr. Christian.

It was from the Langes, just a short note. But with it was a check for one hundred dollars—the promised support from the church. It had come when I needed it, not a day sooner, not a day later.

Down at the airstrip, I paid for my ticket, and flew off to Caracas, not realizing that I would nearly be killed my first day there.

7

Communists

The day before I arrived in Caracas, a state of emergency had been declared—because of demonstrations against the government. I had trouble getting a taxi, and noticed many troops patroling the streets.

The boarding house my friends had directed me to was an old adobe building near the Plaza de Simon Bolivar. The walls were several feet thick, for insulation, even though the temperature only reached a maximum of eighty degrees. I was given a small room with a window on the street.

The house was filled principally with students, and I wasn't long in feeling at home. The narrow halls, illuminated with glass roofing, were painted in bright colors. The "dining room" was a wide point in one of these corridors where a long row of tables had been set up. That night at dinner, when the tables were covered with food and the old straight-backed wooden chairs were filled with arguing students, I was reminded of a carnival.

The next day there was trouble in the streets—much of it almost outside the boarding house door. While I was dressing, I heard a few distant pops. It never occurred to me that they were gunshots. As soon as I stepped out of the boarding-house door, however, I heard the sounds that the thick walls had disguised: the rhythmic chanting of the crowd and the spatter of bullets. I stood frozen in the doorway. Then some soldiers ran around the corner, driving people in front of them. They stopped abruptly. I heard a rat-a-tat-tat from their machine guns, and saw little spurts of dust fly as the bullets hit the dirt that had accumulated on the paved street.

As the action unfolded in front of me, part of me said, "Move, for heaven's sake!" But I stood still, my legs like roots. One of the young men who was running suddenly collapsed—like an untied balloon—and fell face down in the street. The machine guns fired again, and I saw two more people fall, blood oozing from their bodies.

Most of the mob was gone from the street by now, but a few people seemed to hesitate at the corner. One of them, a dark-faced boy with a red bandana around his neck, turned, picked up a rock and ran back toward the troops. He wound up to throw his missile, but as he did, the machine guns, which had been quiet, went rat-a-tat-tat and he seemed to explode: an arm flew off in a red shower and rolled in the dirt.

Then I moved, without first thinking, as though my mind said, "Move," to my body a minute after my body was already moving. I slammed the double door of the house shut, locked and bolted it, then ran up to my room. I shut the window to quiet any sound. I threw myself on the bed. I felt cold. I lay there that way all day, listening to the spatter of the guns.

The next day I had a fever, and remained in bed. When my friends came back to school I was thoroughly sick, with a fever of 103. They got me a doctor. He prescribed some medicine; I didn't ask where it came from because I couldn't pay for it anyway. I later learned that a young man named Lucio Mondragon, a student, had paid for it. He had been stopping in to look at me every day, telling a joke or two, and leaving.

The medicine helped. I was able to move around, although it was some time before I was really well.

As I was convalescing, I struck up a friendship with a local bum and met him each day for an hour of conversation in Spanish. I studied an old Spanish textbook at night.

I shared my room with another student, but after I had been there for two months he moved out. That meant that I had to pay for the room by myself, which was twice as expensive.

Lucio, probably surmising that I didn't have much—if any—money, invited me to move upstairs with him. He even helped me. He was a handsome, thin fellow, with black hair that fell across his forehead, and quick nervous mannerisms. He opened the door to his room, and my first impression was that everything was red. Then I realized that the red was in the shape of hammers and sickles—one entire wall of them!

Lucio walked in and set a box of my things down.

"This is your bed," he said, pointing. "Everything else is at your disposal. Feel free to use the radio." He walked over and switched it on. It was tuned to Radio Havana, from Cuba. Lucio looked up at me, the barest twitch of a smile on his face. "It's best not to try to tune it to different stations. It's very temperamental. It can be difficult to get back on the right station."

It didn't take me long to discover that Lucio was one of the student leaders of the Socialist party on the University campus. Anti-American feeling was strong there, and Lucio constantly tried to aggravate me with it—half in fun, half in submerged fury.

The bum with whom I conversed regularly was quite a character, and wasn't teaching me the best Spanish. My student friends laughed at some of the things I said.

"Your style isn't too good, Olson. Why don't you come to the University where you can really learn?" one asked.

Although attending the University had been beyond my dreams I decided to try it. There weren't many other foreign students there, so a tall, blond American like me stood out like a sore thumb. Soon I was known by most of the students.

It was Lucio and his extremist friends who were kindest to me, however. I could see that their ideals were important to them; that they really wanted to help the poor in their country. I shared their compassion—but we did have some furious arguments.

For example, Lucio always held me directly responsible for whatever the American government did.

"You capitalist pig, he said one day as we sat in a café with a group of other students. "We hope to develop our country, to make it good for the poor as well as for the rich, and what do you Americans do? You come down here and exploit our country, take all the resources out and leave nothing. You dominate our government by paying people off."

"Wait a minute," I said. "I don't do all that."

"Oh, so you don't support your government! Are you a revolutionary?"

"No, I didn't say that."

"Then what are you here for if not for capitalistic reasons? You're a spy, trying to find out how we work so that you can use it against us, just as your government has used it against Vietnam and Cuba. Isn't that right?"

"No," I said. "I'm here because I want to help the Indians, if I can."

The students who had gathered around to listen began to laugh. To them the Indians were not worth enlisting in their political rebellion.

I looked at them with scorn. "And who are you, you elegant Communists, that you can build equality by pulling down the structures and then set up your own that pays no attention to the Indians—the real Venezuelans—who have real needs? Aren't they your people? Or are you as selective as the rich who govern now—to use your own words?"

Lucio always took impossible positions, and baited me with them. It made life tense; I never knew whether he was joking or serious. We were friends, yet there was hate in his life, and some of it often was directed at me.

One day I went swimming with him at Caria del Mar, one of the beautiful beaches on coastal Venezuela. We had argued, and he had called me names. When we got out into the deeper water, we splashed and pushed each other in fun. But there was a grimness in our play that both of us felt.

Suddenly Lucio said, "I'll *kill* you, you capitalist dog." He grabbed me and ducked me under water. At first I didn't struggle. I was sure he would soon let me go. But he didn't. He kept a fierce grip on me. Soon my blood began to pump hard and I felt a terrible urgency to breathe. Still he held me under. I was going to die. I knew it. I fought him with strength I didn't know I had, and finally felt a weakness in his hold. By wrenching with all my strength I got away. Lucio had dived underwater, out of sight. I felt weak and terribly sad. I swam in to the shore and lay down on the sand.

Lucio stayed in the water another twenty minutes, then came over to me. I didn't look up.

"Come on," he said. "Let's get out of here." We walked silently home.

My landlord had never mentioned the rent I owed him, nor had my friends ever asked me to pay my part of the bill when we went to a café for coffee. But it is an uncomfortable feeling to be dependent upon others for everything.

I asked God about it, but received no response. No more money had come from America, and I had no reason to believe it would start coming after all this time. And it was theoretically impossible for me to work for money as a visitor to Venezuela.

One night at a party, however, I met Miguel Nieto, who worked with the ministry of health in Caracas.

"What are you doing in Venezuela?" he asked, then explained that he was looking for someone to teach English to some students who were preparing to attend Harvard's School of Tropical Medicine. "Would you be willing to do it?" he asked.

Was I willing! "But Senor Nieto, I've been told that it is illegal for me to work in Venezuela," I said.

He smiled. "That's okay. We'll pay you in advance. If anything happens, there won't be any contract. We'll just consider it finished business." He stuck a bill into my hand. "Here's your first month's salary. Come see me tomorrow at the Ministry of Health."

I went home so happy I could have danced in the street. I had a job. Soon I would have enough money to pay my bills.

In 1961 President Kennedy and South American presidents met in Punta del Este, Uruguay, to determine U.S.-Latin American policies. It was a period of political tension at the University. Huge, brilliantly-colored posters on most of the buildings opposed cooperation with the United States. One poster showed Uncle Sam as a Pied Piper throwing dollars to the South American presidents, who followed eagerly behind him.

University elections were coming, and Lucio ran on the radical socialist platform. He worked many hours forming a coalition of different socialists. He often came home in the early morning, then would be gone before sunrise.

By this time I had become sympathetic with the goals of the Communist students. I had seen the rude tourists riding in buses and parading down the streets. I had seen the unbecoming behavior of the American embassy staff, and I wasn't proud of them. The Communist students had, at least, a deep concern for their country which ex-patriots never seemed to show for theirs.

Lucio's coalition won the election at the University. "Now you'll see something, Olson, now you'll really see," he said.

He soon found that the worst enemy of a political reformer is winning an election. Within a few months the coalition began to break apart. Few of the students were as committed to it as Lucio; there were squabbles and power struggles, and constant threats to withdraw from it. Lucio finally was forced to admit to failure. One night he threw himself on his bed, cursing.

"Olson, what's the point of all this? No matter how

good my ideas are, someone always ruins them."

That was the first time he had ever asked me for my opinion on anything. I hardly knew how to answer him.

"I know what it is like, Lucio," I said slowly. "Everyone wants you to conform to what they want you to do."

He looked up from his bed. "How do you know what it is like?" he asked. "Have you been a political organizer?"

"No," I said. "But when I first began to follow Jesus, the same kind of thing happened. My father in particular— he is a rich banker, you know—wanted me to go after success, a good job, all the things he thought were important. And my church wanted me to explain everything in the traditional way.

"But Lucio," I said, "it was Jesus that gave me the ability to see beyond all that. That's why I'm here, planning to help Indians. Do you think my father or my friends thought it made sense? They thought I was crazy! They tried to talk me out of it. But Jesus gave me a whole different outlook. He can give you one, too. He can give you the right perspective on life."

"No, no, no," he said. "We've tried Christianity here. It doesn't work. The church is right in with the status quo. They own more land, more business than anyone else in Venezuela—or in all of South America."

We talked late into the night. He knew all the arguments. But he also knew that there was something more to be had in life—something that couldn't be touched—something that could give peace. He sensed it in my life—that peace that wasn't just apathy, that peace which gave me a divine purpose; even an unexplainable power.

Three days later he rushed into the room. "Olson," he said, "Does it really work? Are you telling me the truth?"

"About what?"

"About Jesus. You're not lying to me?"

"No, Lucio. I'm not lying to you."

He sat down quietly and folded his hands.

"All right," he said, looking down on the floor. "All right. I'll do it."

"Do what, Lucio?"

He looked up at me, his face determined. "I'll accept Jesus. I want Him to run my life."

8

Almost Killed

Loneliness plagued me. Often I would walk the streets for hours, just looking at people's faces and trying to overhear their conversations.

You're being silly, I told myself. *You're just a stupid, homesick Minnesotan.* But I didn't want to go back to the States. South America had captivated me.

What I needed was a real friend—one who knew me completely; a brother. I couldn't have put it into words, but the desire was there. And somehow I knew that Lucio would never be that to me.

I also was troubled by my enrollment at the University. I was in South America to help Indians. I had told everyone that. But the University was a funny place to look for Indians.

Miguel Nieto, my superior at the Ministry of Health, knew of my interest in Indians, and called me into his office one day to discuss them.

"Have you ever heard of the Motilone tribe?" he asked.

Our conversation proved to be monumental. Through it I discovered why God had directed me to South America.

The primary contact between the Motilones and civilization came in the form of arrows, Nieto told me. No one had ever learned any of the Motilone language, nor had he even been close enough to describe their physical culture. The Motilones lived in a wild jungle area on the border between Venezuela and Colombia, he said.

Only the big American oil companies seemed to be interested in that area. Everytime their employees entered Motilone territory, however, they were shot at. Great numbers had been wounded by Motilone arrows; many had been killed.

It would have made sense to forget about the Motilones. But I couldn't. A gnawing, troubling curiosity grabbed me. And it wouldn't go away, no matter how good the arguments I used against it.

What on earth can I do for a bunch of savage, primitive Indians? I asked myself.

It didn't matter what I thought I could do. In my innermost self I somehow *knew* that God wanted me to go to them. But I was afraid, and tried to talk my way out of committing myself. I had forgotten how hard God can make it on someone who won't do what he's told. I lost my ability to concentrate, to do anything but think about the Motilones.

Even so, I wasn't going to go!

I was sitting in the Ministry of Health one day, waiting to see an official, when a passerby tossed a newspaper onto the seat next to me. I glanced over at it.

The word "Motilone" caught my eye. I looked more closely. An article reported that an epidemic of measles was affecting a large number of the Motilones. An oil company employee had discovered more than twenty dead—and deserted—in one of their communal homes. His description of their rotting bodies was detailed and chilling.

Somewhere inside me a cord snapped. What was I fighting against? Why the resistance? There people were in need. I had studied tropical medicine; I might be able to help.

Within a week I was on a bus for Machiques, a town in the foothills of the Andes. I had not gotten off easily: visa problems had taken me clear to the president of the country. And it had been hard to leave my student friends. They were sure I was crazy.

Still, I felt cheerful. The bus was crowded, not only with people, but with livestock. I ended up carrying a large pig on my lap for most of the three-day trip. I was much more at ease than when I had left Caracas to go up the Orinoco, however. I now spoke Spanish quite well, and enjoyed talking to the other passengers. A fat, red-faced rancher's wife riding with me had heard of the Motilones, and I pumped her for information. She told me many colorful stories about people being wounded by their long, heavy arrows.

"Don't you go near them," she said, shaking a big finger. "They'll kill you."

I got the same advice from a number of people in Machiques. But I was confident—and excited at beginning a new adventure. I also vividly remembered my trip up the Orinoco. Those Indians had been so friendly, so wonderful to live with. In my mind, Indians were Indians. Getting along in the jungle shouldn't be too hard either. After all, I'd done it on the Orinoco.

I had saved enough money to buy supplies, and decided to start off with a short visit, perhaps of a week. The only transportation into the Andes from Machiques is on foot, so I bought a mule, a "real sure-footed" one, according to the man who sold it to me. The two of us set out early one morning on the trail I had been told to take.

The trail was easy to follow as it gradually climbed up into the Andes. I expected at any moment to meet a friendly Motilone Indian and be taken to his village.

I rode rather jauntily all day, pausing only to snack on some bread. As the sun got lower and the beautiful varied greens of the jungle got darker I began to feel tired. Disappointed that I hadn't met any Indians, and that I would have to spend the night outside, I kept pushing the mule along, hoping to come to an Indian village.

Suddenly I stopped. I had missed the trail. Ahead were

only vines and creepers. I backtracked until I found the trail. But I didn't go very far on it. Within a hundred yards it disappeared again.

I went back. It was strange that I would take two wrong turns in a row. I hadn't had any trouble following it before. Perhaps it was just the difference in the light.

The trail no longer was well marked. It had become a thin, weedy path through the trees. When I picked it up again, I followed it carefully. But I hadn't gone more than a few yards before I realized that there was no path at all!

I crisscrossed the area, pulling the tired and now stubborn mule after me through bushes and vines. There was no sign of a trail. It had vanished.

I stood and looked around me, my heart pounding. There was nothing on all sides but silent, dark trees and vines. They all looked alike.

I tried to remember my Boy Scout training. How did a Boy Scout figure out where he was? I couldn't recall.

I knew what I could do. I could wait until the sun rose the next morning and get my directions from it.

That thought relieved me. It was simple. Just wait until morning.

But in what direction had I been traveling? Where was Machiques from here? I thought I had been going east, but I wasn't sure.

It was now quite dark. I could see only the silhouettes of the trees. I had nothing to sleep in. I would have to lie down on the ground. At least it wasn't cold.

I tied up the mule, picked out a spot, and lay down. In the process of squirming back and forth to find a more comfortable position, I got a thorn stuck in my back side. I sat up in a hurry.

I was unhappy, tired and depressed. Did I really know what I was doing? The jungle that had seemed so pleasant during the day began to seem dangerous. I heard scurrying, thrashing noises in the bushes. Strange, wailing screams bit into the air. I couldn't sleep.

I kept waiting for the sun to come up. The night seemed hours longer than it should be. Once, when I was on the verge of drifting off to sleep, something landed on my face and immediately hopped off into the brush. Adrenaline pumped through my veins. I was wide awake.

I watched the darkness turn into a gray which gradually got lighter. When I could distinguish colors, I got up. I was stiff, and had a horrible taste in my mouth.

I had a can of sardines left from my lunch, and a candle to heat them with. The thought of food made me ravenously hungry, for I had neglected to eat the night before. I hurriedly rustled through my pack until I found the can.

But I had forgotten to pack a can opener.

I got out my knife and started to cut the can. My knife broke. From the little hole I had opened, I greedily sucked the olive juice. I had to eat! I couldn't go without food! I might starve.

I tried banging the can on a rock, but it didn't do any good. Finally I tossed it into the bushes.

I had wasted an hour. I still didn't have my bearings. Nor did I have any idea how to find the trail on which I had come in. But I didn't want to go back.

The sun was coming up over a mountain in the distance. I decided that I would go in that direction. I started off, pulling my reluctant mule after me. Now that there was no path it was slow going. The mule constantly got tangled in hanging vines and creepers. Some of the bushes had long thorns, and several of them stuck into my hands and legs. The cuts puffed up hideously after I pulled the thorns out. I began to feel feverish.

As I climbed higher into the mountains the foliage thinned out, and beautiful iridescent blue butterflies flew everywhere. Flaming red parrots squawked at me. The air got cooler. My hunger had disappeared, but I felt weak. Bugs continued to bite me, as they had ever since I began the trip. Every exposed area of my body was covered with red welts.

That night I did sleep, although nightmares woke me several times. It was cold, and I didn't have warm clothes to cover me. When I got up in the morning the first thing that I did was retch. I looked at my hands, and hardly recognized them for what they were. They were red and swollen, bit up like a piece of raw meat.

"Why, Lord?" I asked. "What am I doing here?" But I untied my mule and continued. The hills were too steep to ride him, so I pulled him along, stumbling, barely in control of myself.

Then, looking across a deep valley to the ridge on the other side, I saw a cluster of huts. It was an Indian village. I blinked.

Thank God. I had found the Motilones.

I worked my way down the valley, then slowly, tediously up the other side. It took several hours. I kept looking ahead of me, expecting to see some Indians. Then, because my eyes weren't looking at my feet, I would trip and fall.

Finally I reached the circle of huts. I felt a great surge of relief as a group of people came down toward me.

"I'm here!" I shouted, not caring whether they could understand or not.

Twenty or more Indians surrounded me, staring and jabbering in their own language. I tried speaking to them in Spanish. No response. I tried the few Indian phrases I had learned during my stay in the Orinoco. Still no response.

All the people seemed old and wrinkled. They looked at me, poked me and laughed. Most were missing teeth. When they opened their mouths, their red toothless gums showed.

We walked into the village. There women and children came out to look at me. No one understood a word I said. They didn't even try to listen.

I was sure there must be a chief. Perhaps he and the young men were out hunting. I kept looking up, expecting them to arrive. But they didn't come, and I got tired of standing in the middle of this circle of smiling, senile old folks, women and children. I still felt sick and dizzy.

What could I do to communicate? Then I remembered the small wooden flute I had brought along to amuse myself. Perhaps these people would be interested in hearing me play it.

I got it out of my pack, sat down, and began to play. As I did, almost everyone nodded in time to the music. When I stopped, one old fellow put his hands in front of his mouth, making the motions of playing, as though to indicate I should play some more. So I struck up a tune I had learned from the Indians on the Orinoco River. Another man suddenly produced a flute and copied the line I had played. I gave him a second line, and he copied that one too. Soon we were playing the song together.

Then he played a melody I'd never heard before. I copied him, line for line. By this time, the whole village had stopped to listen.

Our playing went on and on. I began to get tired, but no one got up to leave. Finally, at three-thirty in the morning, we quit.

It rained heavily that night. I lay awake in the hut I had been taken to, listening to the heavy breathing of the men who were with me. At least I was in a safe place, with people who seemed friendly.

The next morning there was still no sign of a chief. I was given a breakfast of rough, boiled roots and horrible-tasting liquid. I forced them down; I was hungry enough to eat anything.

No one seemed interested in continuing the flute concert, but left me for their own projects. The little children played games. One old fellow sat in the sun, leaning against one of the huts. When I looked over at him he smiled back.

I walked over to him. "How are you?" I asked in English.

He started talking in his own language, which is what I wanted. I mimicked what he had said.

He laughed, said some more words, and I tried to repeat them. Again he laughed. The game seemed to delight him, and we continued for at least two hours. It was my first experience in trying to understand a language without having any clues. Fascinated, I soon forgot everything else. I was beginning to be able to separate some of of the sounds, and it was just a question of time, I thought, before I began to get the meaning of some of the words.

Suddenly, without warning, a blow hit my back and

knocked me onto my face. I lay stunned. A man was standing over me, yelling and wailing at a terrific pitch, slashing at me with whips which he held in each hand. White froth dripped from his lips. I tried to roll away from his blows, but several young men appeared and poked me back toward him with long, sharp arrows which they held in their hands.

Then, at the man's direction, I was picked up by two of the warriors and thrown into the hut in which I had spent the night. No one came in after me. I lay on the floor, panting, almost terrified. Welts were rising on my arms and legs where the whip had hit them.

An arrow slashed through one grass wall of the hut and hit the wall on the other side. Other arrows followed. The men had surrounded the hut and were shooting at me through it. The arrows didn't have enough force to break my skin by the time they came through the walls, but they were heavy, and made ugly bruises and blood blisters where they hit. After fifteen minutes of this I collapsed on the floor, my hands over my eyes.

The man who had used the whip came to the door of the hut and shouted at me. By this time I had figured out that he was the chief. He now had a long arrow in his bow, and looked insane. I hugged the ground, begging in English, "Please, don't. Don't. Please don't."

He left the doorway. There was a long pause, and hope surged through me. Then I heard a "pphhhht," and an arrow blinded me with pain. As the arrows continued to fly, the scene became unreal. It seemed the kind of thing that happens only in movies.

At the moment of my greatest terror, it occurred to me that I needed to pray.

"God," I said, "how long is this going to go on? Do I have to go through this?" I could imagine a future filled with torture, inability to communicate, and death.

Then a strange thing happened. It was as though I were struck down. I seemed to see Jesus on the cross. I started to cry.

"Oh, Jesus," I said, astonished and fearful. "That's what *You* faced. We must have seemed filthy to You, like these Indians seem to me. Oh, how senseless our hate must have been."

I lay quietly. "God, I will give You what I can. I give You my strength, my life. I'll put up with anything, any trouble. I'll even die, if You will let me communicate about Your Son to the Motilones."

Perhaps I had prayed that prayer before. This time, though, I meant it. Thinking death was near, I had to mean it.

A few more arrows hit me, but I was no longer terrified of them. After a while the chief was restrained by some older men. Later I learned that he had been drunk—a condition he and the other Indians of the tribe often were in.

I got out my flute again, and began to play. I had left it in the hut overnight. Its mellow sound was a comfort, and seemed to make the pain in my arms and legs less severe. Soon someone outside began to play with me.

But the chief made it clear that I was not welcome in the village. There was no reason why I shouldn't leave. I packed up my belongings, got on my mule, and started back toward Machiques.

Just as I was about to enter the jungle below the village, an old man called to me. He signaled that I was to wait, and disappeared into one of the huts. He came out carrying a child.

I went back to look at the child. He was a boy, perhaps four years old, who appeared very sick. Some of the other villagers, seeing me look at the child, brought out other children, who seemed to have the same disease. A circle of concerned, sad faces formed around me.

I had a small vial of an antibiotic with me but I hesitated to use it. It was six months past the expiration date. However, these children might die if they didn't get some kind of medical attention. So I got out the medicine and began to administer it. There wasn't enough for all the children, so I gave a half dose. I had no confidence that this would help them, but it was all that I could do.

I unpacked my mule and waited to see the result. I asked God to heal the children where the medicine couldn't. A day passed, and there was no change in their condition. But the day after that, one child began to look better. A few hours later all were showing encouraging signs. Within a week they were playing happily.

The chief changed his attitude toward me. He could see that I was interested in helping his tribe. Later, I learned that the day he had found me in his village, two of his young men had been shot to death by white settlers. So he had reason to dislike me.

My visit stretched on. I began to learn the language. Soon I realized that these were not Motilone Indians. None of the descriptions of the Motilones matched up with this culture.

These Indians called themselves Yukos. I wasn't to contact the Motilones for another year. And my reception was to be even more fearful.

9
Bribery

I finished packing the mule, and walked around him making sure that all the cinch straps were tight. A small huddle of Yukos watched me. I looked uncertainly at them. Should I do more than say goodbye? Should I shake hands or hug each one? The Yukos looked stolidly at me, no sign of emotion on their faces.

I held up a hand. "Goodbye." I said. "I'm sorry to go."

Liar, I told myself.

I got on the mule and rode off, looking back once to wave.

I turned the mule onto the rocky, steep trail that led out of the village. I'd been told it would take me to civilization.

Well, I'd done more than my share. I could be satisfied with that. After all, what had begun as a week-long visit had lasted four months.

Boy, would it be nice to get out to civilization and talk to someone who understood English. And food. My mouth watered for a coke or a hamburger. The Yuko food was awful. Day after day, always the same. Corn and chicha. Chicha was an alcoholic drink made by chewing corn and spitting it into a big gourd, then letting it ferment. It tasted about as good as it sounds.

It was a cold and misty day. The peaks around the village were obscured by clouds. I'd never expected to want to go back to the warmer, wet jungles of the lower elevations. But four months of constant shivering were getting to me.

It's stupid to feel guilty about leaving, I thought to myself. I was sick. For two months I had been passing blood. I needed medical attention.

The mule kept plodding along, taking me farther from the Yukos.

Boredom had become my greatest enemy. I could take having arrows shot at me. At least that was over quickly. But getting up each day to the same food, to the same filthy smell, to the same people with whom I had no rapport: that really got me. So it was time to leave. I'd done my part. So what if no one had come to know Christ. I had learned enough of their language to tell them about Him. I had done what I could.

The mule took me slowly down one slope, and up a high ridge. The man who had sold it to me hadn't lied. It was a good, sure-footed animal. If this trail really went out of the jungle, like the Indians said it did, we would get out.

Suddenly the mule reared. I tried to hold on, but couldn't. I was thrown into the air. My hands clawed for something to grab onto, but the mule was gone from underneath me. I landed heavily on my right shoulder as I heard the mule galloping off through the underbrush.

I stood up slowly. My shoulder had been wrenched in the fall. It hurt. My pack had broken open, and my belongings were strewn along the trail. I was only an hour out of the village, but I hated to go back. I could go ahead on foot, hoping to make it, but I really needed that mule, and he was on his way back to the village. I would have to go there, too.

It was a long walk back, and my shoulder hurt badly.

Even worse was the emotional difficulty of returning to a place I'd just abandoned. Somehow I didn't want to see those Indians again.

My worst fears were realized when I came into the village. The people had seen the mule long before I got there, so they knew what had happened. They came to meet me, laughing! The great white man had been felled by a mule. No one helped me carry my pack.

I was tired from the walk, and my shoulder was stiff, but I wasn't going to stay and be laughed at. I saddled the mule, packed him up, and left again.

This time things went better. It was odd that the mule had bucked and thrown me. Mules weren't supposed to do that. And this one was particularly good-tempered.

I went along for about three hours, and was feeling better. Soon I would be in civilization.

Suddenly the mule stopped dead, and put down his head. I tightened up on the reins, as I had been told to do. But the mule kicked up and threw me over his head. I landed in a cold, mucky puddle. The mule hadn't run, however, so I stood up to try to catch him. He reared up and kicked at me, his hoof hitting my arm and then my face. Blood spurted out of my mouth, down my neck and onto my clothes. The pain was blinding. I wished I could pass out, but the pain just built up and up into a solid wall that seemed like a vibrating shell all round me.

When the pain subsided enough so that I could see, the mule was gone. I put pressure on my mouth to stop the blood.

I couldn't go back to the village. I had to leave this jungle. I would walk out. But not now. It was late. I could spend the night here, and go on in the morning.

That night I shivered and slept only fitfully. The whole side of my jaw was swollen out of shape.

In the morning I felt terrible, and knew I would have to go back to the village. I wondered what God was trying to tell me through all this.

The Yukos did not like me. They were as happy as I when I left. So why couldn't I leave? Why had God twice let me be thrown from the mule?

Then I remembered the mission board and the lesson I had learned from it. The mission had rejected me, but God hadn't. Now it was happening again. The Yukos didn't particularly want me to stay, but God did. And I would have to follow God.

The sun was bright that day. I felt feverish and dizzy. Before long the sun seemed to be baking me. My clothes were stiff with mud and dried blood. My head felt light.

I stumbled along. When I reached the bottom of one valley I found a stream that I had barely noticed before. I lowered myself into it and lay in the cool water, letting it soften my clothes and skin. I stayed there without moving for at least an hour.

When I got up, it was late afternoon. I knew I had to make it to the village before nightfall. I felt weak, too weak to even stand. Time after time I fell down and lay still for minutes before gathering the strength to get up again.

As I neared the village, I began to yell, "Help me, please help me." By that time I didn't care if they laughed.

Suddenly a few Yukos did appear. The chief was with them. They didn't laugh.

The chief himself carried me up to the village and helped take care of me. It was a week before I felt well enough to get up. When I did, I no longer wanted to leave. The Indians had become people to me. They had cared for me when I needed help. Now I would stay and see if I could help them.

Not that it was any easier. Life was still boring there. I still had amoebic dysentery, and I still passed blood every morning. But I did make progress with the language, and soon was able to speak reasonably well. That helped greatly. The more I spoke the more I began to understand these people, and the more I understood the more I wanted to help them. What had seemed ignorance or stupidity, didn't seem like that now.

It was something I would need to remember many times: Before you really understand a people, don't judge.

But I still wanted to get to the Motilones. Of course, it was too late to help with the measle epidemic. But that didn't mean I shouldn't go there. Gradually that desire, which had been so strong before I had met the Yukos, reasserted itself.

I asked the Yukos about the tribes around them. One tribe stood out in their minds, a tribe that they warred with. The Yukos knew them as the "people of the oil." That made sense; the Motilone region was so rich in oil that there were natural seepages in parts of it. From that and their other descriptions I soon was convinced that the "people of the oil" were the Motilones.

I asked the Yukos if they would take me to the Motilones. Their eyes opened wide with horror.

"Oh, no, we don't go near them. They'd kill us," one said.

I insisted.

"Well," he said, "there is a Yuko tribe south of here. Maybe they will take you. You can try there."

This time leaving was not so hard. God really did want me to go, even though I still hadn't accomplished anything great. Not one of the Yukos had come to know Christ. I hadn't been able to offer any improvements in their way of life. I hadn't even been able to feel at home in their culture. There was unfinished business there, but I felt an urgency to be with the Motilones—an urgency that could come only from God.

So I said goodbye and went down to live with the southern tribe. I didn't expect to be there long, but the moment I tried to speak with one of them I found that I was in for a bit of trouble. These Yukos spoke a different dialect. I couldn't understand them.

But they were friendly. They took me in and let me eat and sleep with them. After a month I had learned enough of their language to ask them about taking me to the Motilones.

They looked terrified. "Oh, no, we don't go near them. Maybe the tribe east of here will take you to them."

I began going from tribe to tribe, trying to get someone to take me. Sometimes I thought of striking out by myself, but I had learned enough about the jungle not to try that again.

In each tribe it was always "someone else" who might take me. Once I did get a group to go with me, but after just one day on the trail I got violently ill and had to go back. At first I thought that perhaps I was going against God's will, as I had when He'd used the mule to make me go back. On second thought I knew that this time I was right. I wasn't going to the Motilones for the sake of my own comfort. I was going because I had felt the call of God. So I persisted.

I had my eye on one young Yuko. He was strong, a great one to laugh and have a good time. He had a reputation for being willing to do anything if there was something he could get from it.

I had a card up my sleeve. The Yukos love bright things, and the first tribe I'd stayed with had been fascinated by my zippers. My western-style clothes had long since worn out, and I was wearing the traditional poncho of the Yukos. But I had saved the zipper from my trousers, and kept it in the bottom of my pack.

After two months of waiting, I got it out and tied it to a piece of string. Then I drew the young man aside. I led him secretively into the jungle, then pulled out the zipper. I let it dangle from the string so that the sun caught it and made it sparkle.

He grabbed for it, but I pulled it away. "I'll give you this if you take me to the Motilones," I said.

I watched the conflict. Every time he thought about going near the Motilones he frowned and drew back. But every time he looked at the zipper he wanted it more.

Finally he shrugged. "Sure. Why not?"

I grabbed him by the shoulders. "Great! We leave tomorrow?"

He nodded, glumly.

10

A Terrifying Reception

Seven of us set out early the next day at a fast trot. The sun was just coming up over the mountains as we left the village, and the air was fresh and cool.

We seldom spoke. We pushed on all day, following almost invisible trails over mountain ridges, choosing forks in the trail without consultation. We didn't stop to eat. When the sun went down we walked until we could no longer see the trail. The next morning we were travelling before the sun came up.

We went at that grinding pace for six days. Gradually the landscape and climate changed. The sparse trees of the high Andes became the tall, close trees of the tropical jungle. Vines hung from trees, some as thick as ropes. Even the sounds were different. Parrots screamed at us. Sometimes a monkey screeched as it swung from tree to tree to avoid us.

Each day I collapsed on the ground when we finally made our stop. Each day it became harder to get up in the morning dark. The Yukos, however, showed no sign of tiring. The heat annoyed them, and sweat streamed down their faces as they walked, but they didn't slow their pace.

We were heading for a ridge in Motilone territory that they told me overlooked a Motilone home. There they would leave me to fend for myself. As we drew closer to the home, the Yukos became more and more quiet. Once I started to comment about a bright-colored parrot I had seen, and immediately felt a hand clapped across my mouth. It was one of the Yukos. There was no smile on his face. Only when he was sure that I wouldn't say anything did he take his hand away from my mouth.

We no longer had to climb the towering Andes. Here there were only small bluffs and ridges. The trees were so thick we seldom saw the sky. Rivers were the problem. Often the ground was swampy near the banks, so that it sometimes took hours to work out a safe route across. On the seventh day of the trip we woke up and began to walk without a word. I knew that we were near the Motilone ridge and, tired as I was, there was a little more spring to my step.

This is what I had come to the jungle for. I soon was going to see my first Motilone.

Suddenly all the Yukos stopped and raised their heads as if to sniff the wind. They stood like statues. I hadn't heard a sound, but I stood still too, listening to my breath come hard and loud—too loud, I thought. I heard nothing else.

Then, as if in one motion, all the Yukos broke into a run, back the way we had come. I stood stunned for a moment, then, clumsily, ran after them, wondering what I was running for. I ran straight into some vines, tripped, and fell flat on my face, scrambled up, and got tangled in the vines again. Then a searing pain bit into my thigh, and my whole body went limp. I fell.

Everything seemed to move slowly—even my huge, gulping breaths. I looked down at my thigh. A long shaft was sticking out of it, with a neat little punch-hole where the arrow had gone in. The hole was a bright red from the blood, *my* blood, oozing out and down my leg.

I couldn't take my eyes off the arrow. It seemed unreal. It had to be sticking out from someone else's leg. But it wasn't.

Then I looked up, and my heart almost stopped. I was encircled by dark-skinned, naked men, with huge bows drawn taut. Nine little dots of arrowheads pointed right at me. I forgot all about my leg.

"Don't shoot, don't!" I said in Yuko, pleading also with my eyes. Their eyes, like little black chunks of coal, made no response. Their arms did not relax at their bows.

"Oh, please," I said in Spanish, "I come as a friend.

"Friend," I said in Latin.

Without taking their eyes off me, they removed the arrows from their bows. One of the men walked over to me. I cowered. He reached down to my leg and grasped the arrow by the shaft. Putting his foot on my thigh, he yanked out the arrow. I saw little red, dancing stars. I couldn't breathe. I looked down at my leg and saw a bit of my muscle trailing in the blood from where the arrow had been pulled. Every second the pain seemed to be more than I could stand, and then, unbelievably, it got worse.

The man took the arrow and poked me in the back. I tried to ignore him. I wanted only to lie there and die. He insisted. He wanted me to stand. I did. Then he poked me in the back and I stumbled ahead. The other men formed a file, and we began to walk back into Motilone territory.

The march lasted three hours. My leg pained beyond description, but every time I began to slow down I felt the arrow point in my back.

We went up a long, steep hill, and I knew I couldn't go much farther before I fainted. A dark throb in the corner of my eyes threatened to take over my whole field of vision. My leg felt as though it had been cut almost in half.

Finally we broke into sunlight at the top of the hill, and I saw a huge brown mound in the middle of a rough clearing. It looked like a beehive, planted unnaturally on the ground. It stood about forty feet high, and there were dark, rectangular holes at the ground level.

We went straight to it, and entered one of the dark holes, stooping to get in. It was too dark to see at first. I heard little woman-screams, scuffling, and the cries of children. Gradually my eyes got used to the dim light. I was shoved down onto a little mat.

The women and children were gone. Only men stood over me, looking fierce and dangerous in the shadows. Suddenly the statistics of murdered oil-company employees seemed very real. Had they brought me here to kill me?

The men talked, then backed away and left me alone. I looked around at the building. It wasn't round as I had thought, but oblong. There were six doors. Palm-tree trunks had been bent in from the ground and tied to form a beautiful, simple arch framework, then covered with brown palm leaves. My eyes went back and forth across them. They seemed to get lighter, then to move gently, as though a breeze were swaying them. I felt relaxed. I couldn't feel the hurt in my legs. Just before I passed out I realized what was happening, and I laughed.

"I'm delirious," I said out loud. "How about that?" And I laughed again.

I think I awoke the next day. There was no way of knowing how long I had been unconscious. The women and children were paying no attention to me. I felt hot and feverish. My thigh was swollen, and ugly yellow pus surrounded the place where the arrow had gone in.

I propped myself up on my elbow, but began to feel dizzy, so I lay back down and looked at the ceiling. The high arches were almost like a cathedral's. The quiet murmur of the women doing their work sounded like prayers.

I had diarrhea. The first time I felt its urging I tried to stand up by myself to walk outside. I was quickly shoved back down to my mat. We finally worked out a series of signals so that one of the women could accompany me just outside the door where the Indians defecated. I did the same, red-faced, because the woman watched me carefully. My trips out of necessity became more and more frequent.

I lay on the mat all day, half-awake. The glands under my arms were beginning to swell. No food was offered me. Late in the afternoon I was awakened from a doze by what sounded like war-whoops. I sat up, expecting the worst. The men streamed in, yelling and holding up monkeys and parrots which they had shot. Excited conversation filled the air. They held the animals over the fire to burn off the feathers or fur. The house was filled with acrid, choking smoke. Then the women cooked the animals.

I was extremely hungry, even though my fever made me feel sick to my stomach. But I was offered none of the food. That night when all the Motilones had strung up hammocks and were sleeping, I lay awake, sweating, the room threatening to sway and turn over in my head. My thigh ached clear to the bone. It obviously was infected, and I couldn't even wash it. I started to cry from weakness. The tears were somehow comforting.

Then I began to pray, and I prayed as I hadn't for a long time. I spoke quietly to God, my eyes open and watching the slightly-moving hammocks of the Motilones strung high off the ground. God comforted me. I was doing, He let me know, what He wanted.

The next afternoon a little boy came up to me with a palm leaf folded in his hand. He smiled and held out the leaf. In it was a mess of squirming grubs. Each was about the size and shape of a hot dog.

I didn't know what to do. I shrugged my shoulders and put a puzzled expression on my face.

One of the grubs wriggled off the leaf and fell to the ground. The boy quickly reached down, picked it up, bit off its head, then chewed and swallowed the rest of the grub.

He held out the leaf again. I was supposed to eat the grub. A wave of nausea swept through me. But I was hungry, and if I refused to eat these, who knew when I would be offered food again?

I reached out tentatively and picked up one of the smallest grubs. It writhed in my hand. I shut my eyes, put its head between my teeth, bit it off and quickly spit it out. The insides of the worm pushed up out of its body. I knew that if I looked at them I wouldn't be able to eat, so I popped the whole thing in my mouth, and chewed. It was like rubber. The flavor wasn't bad: a little like bacon. I picked up another and ate it, then another.

My stomach revolted. My skin went cold. I could feel the worms churning in my stomach. Suddenly they came up the way they'd gone down.

When I at last looked up, the boy had left. Later he brought me some smoked fish, and I was able to eat them and keep them down. From then on I was given plenty to eat, and no more grubs.

I got sicker. The days seemed to float by. I was still not allowed to leave my mat, but I doubted whether I could have stood up to leave anyway. The glands under one of my arms was so swollen I couldn't put my arm all the way down. My thigh was not healing.

When I could stay awake I watched the women doing their chores, or the men making arrows. Most of the men seemed cruel. They poked me and laughed when I jumped. One fellow, though, seemed to have taken it into his head to protect me. Whenever he came up the others would move away. He had a loud distinctive laugh—was funny to look at, too. He walked pigeon-toed, and there was a little scar by the side of his mouth. Every day when he came back from hunting, he smiled and said something to me. Often it was he who brought me food.

I was there a month, living a kind of half-life. My diarrhea got worse. I was so weak that I could hardly sit up. I had to be helped outside.

One day I knew that I had to leave. God wanted me to, I felt sure.

But that meant losing my contact with the Motilones. How could I give that up after all it had taken me to get it? On the other hand, what good would it be to me if I were dead?

That night the moon was out. I could see it shining outside the house. I stood up quietly, teetering a little because of my dizziness. No one moved to stop me. Everyone was asleep.

I tiptoed to the door. Still no one stirred. I stepped out into the night air, my heart beating hard from fear. For a moment I even forgot I was sick.

A path led downhill from the door. I wanted to get to water to disguise my tracks. My leg hurt where the arrow had struck it, and it was stiff, so I had to drag it along. The path was rough; rocks jabbed into my feet.

When I got to the bottom of the mountain I stopped. There was a small river. I bathed my leg. The water stung, bringing tears to my eyes. I listened for sounds of being followed. There were none.

I had to follow the river, either up or down, or I would get lost. Upriver, I knew, I would come to the mountains. On the other side would be settlements. Downriver, I didn't know what I would find. So I went upriver.

For four days I walked without food. I saw nothing from the bank that I was sure was edible, and I was afraid of the many poisonous plants in the jungle. Fever burned in me. I felt alternately hot and cold. It was a terrific effort just to lift up my feet. Sometimes I waded. Other times I walked the rocky bank.

The river snaked its way up into the mountains. Often I had to cross it to find a way up over the rocks. Sometimes the icy current would catch me, pick me up and bang me against rocks and boulders before I could struggle out of it. It would have been easier to let the river carry me away.

My feet were swollen from climbing on the jagged rocks. Several times I was blocked by a waterfall with cliffs on either side, and I had to climb up the slick, mossy boulders, pawing for handholds to keep me from falling.

On the afternoon of the fifth day I wearily dropped into a seat between two huge boulders. I leaned back, resting my body against the damp, cold rock.

I looked at my fingernails, blue from the cold water; at my hands and fingers, pale white. My whole body groaned with pain; my stomach ached with hunger. I started to shake, and couldn't stop. I stared at the water, my gaze out of focus. The rushing water seemed to stand still.

Could I go any farther? I didn't see how. I needed food, rest. Something on the surface of the water seemed to be waving up and down, bright yellow. I couldn't make my eyes focus on it. I thought I was delirious. I rubbed my eyes. The water came into focus. Bobbing along in the current was a stalk of bananas. I grabbed them as they floated by. I couldn't believe it. They were ripe, too: unripe bananas are terribly bitter.

I had a hard time keeping them down, but as I began to digest them I felt them giving me strength and new hope.

I got up, and began to walk upriver. In a few hours the river reached a high basin, where it petered out into several little streams. I climbed up the wall of the basin and finally reached the top of the mountains.

I could see down the forested slopes of the area ahead. Nowhere was there a sign of life. Nowhere was there a break in the trees—only miles and miles of the same jungle I had just come through.

I collapsed on a fallen log. What was the point of going on? Even if there were a settlement somewhere out there, how would I ever find it?

Every day since my escape I had thought, *If I can just get to the top of the mountains I will be safe.* Now I saw that I wasn't any better off than before. There was no safety anywhere.

Then I thought about the bananas. Had God given them to me to mock me, to make me think there was hope and then take it away?

I remembered the words, "Thou preparest a table before me in the presence of mine enemies." God had given me a table in the middle of the jungle, a table of ripe bananas. Would He forget me now?

Somewhere out there, I thought, looking at the miles of unbroken trees, *there must be people who can help me. God showed me the banana stalk when I needed it. He can take me to those people.*

I won't say that I had complete confidence that He'd

do that. But I did pull my aching, sick body off of the log and start walking again.

I found a streambed in the valley below and began to follow it down. I was in a daze. I seemed to be having a bad dream from which I couldn't wake up. All day I walked down the river bed. Sometimes I would rather have lain down and let the water carry me away. But I kept going.

I didn't recognize the sound at first. It was high, sharp—like that of a woodpecker, only louder and slower. I listened carefully, thinking what an odd sound it was to hear in the jungle. Something deep in my mind told me it was important. Some memory stirred, but I couldn't give it a name. It was a noise I'd heard before.

I decided to investigate. As I got closer I remembered. It was the sound of an axe on a tree. A human being!

Had God done it? Had He brought me to some civilization?

I trotted toward the sound, stumbling, my legs barely working in a loose shambling run. Then I saw two men cutting at the base of a huge tree. As I shouted at them, I lost my balance and fell into the dirt.

11

In and Out of Civilization

"Who's that?" one of the men yelled, probably thinking I was an Indian. I had fallen behind a bush, so they couldn't see me.

"Help me!" I cried. "Please help!"

They stopped their work and came over to look at me.

"What's the problem here?" one of them asked.

"Doctor," was all I could gasp out.

They looked at each other with puzzled expressions then picked me up and propped me against a tree. They gave me a corn patty and some sugar. I opened my mouth to thank them, but found I couldn't talk. It took a long time to eat the corn patty. I was too weak to chew well.

The men got a mule, put me on it and took me to a nearby house. One of their wives brought me some good red beans, two more corn patties, and a cup of rich, sweet coffee. I began to feel stronger. While I stuffed the food in my mouth I asked them how far I was from Machiques.

"Machiques? Never heard of it."

I was surprised. Machiques was a well-known town.
"What is the nearest town?" I asked.

"Talamaque."

"How far is that?" I'd never heard of it.

"A good two days . . . walking."

"And what's the next largest town?"

"Rincon Honda."

"What? Colombia? I'm in Colombia?"

I didn't take time to ponder it. A few minutes later I
fell asleep. I woke up in a bed, the first bed I had seen
in more than a year. The sun was coming in the window
at about the same angle as when I had fallen asleep.
I've slept only a few minutes, I thought. Then I realized
that it must be the next day.

I got up, washed and dressed. I felt better, although
I was still weak. I looked in the mirror. I was like a scare-
crow! My clothes—which I had gotten from the Yukos—
were in tatters. No wonder the men had been a little
frightened.

That day I rested quietly. My body wasn't used to food,
so I ate only small amounts. Otherwise I started to feel
sick. I got a map and tried to figure out where I had
been during the last year.

The next day the colonists took me to Talamaque.
I had some Venezuelan money that I had managed to keep
the whole time I was in the jungle. I exchanged it for
Colombian pesos, went to a clothing store, and bought a
good pair of shoes, khaki slacks, and a shirt. Leaving my
filthy, tattered clothes in the store dressing room, I
walked out into the street feeling like a new man.

I wanted to get out of the frontier and go to Bogota,
the capital of Colombia. There I could get my bearings.
I didn't have enough money to get there, so I bought a
train ticket for about half the distance. That left me penniless. But I didn't worry about how I would get the rest
of the way. Somehow it would work out.

It was great to sit on the train and let it carry me, without effort, without worry. I had never appreciated a train
before. The speed seemed incredibly fast. I put my legs
on the seat opposite me and relaxed.

Halfway through the trip the train was stopped, and some military men got on. They started moving through the car I was in, checking everyone's papers.

"Hey, what are they doing?" I asked a man across the car from me.

He shrugged. "They're looking for Communist guerillas. Sometimes they catch them on the trains."

A short, stocky soldier with a large, bushy moustache came up to me. "May I see your identification, please?"

I shook my head. "I haven't any. I'm sorry."

"You haven't any? Why?"

"I just came out of the jungle."

Heads turned to stare at me. The soldier looked stern. "You'd better come with me," he said.

He took me to his commander, who didn't believe my story, either. I was taken off the train. The commander wired Bogota that he had captured a suspicious expatriot who appeared to have been in the jungle.

I was escorted to a military post where I was fed a good square meal. Then the commander told me that he would have to send me on to Bogota for questioning.

All I did was shrug. Underneath I was laughing. I had no money, and a train ticket that went only halfway to my destination. Now the military was feeding me and sending me to where I wanted to go! I had a Friend in high places.

In Bogota I told my story to a number of top-ranking officials. They didn't believe all of it, but I did convince them that I had been in the jungle. They wired the U.S. embassy which, of course, had never heard of me, since I wasn't registered in Colombia. I couldn't convince the officials that they should check in Venezuela. They were sure that part of my story was false.

"No one," they said, "enters Motilone territory and comes out alive."

Thinking to trip me, they sent me to Dr. Gregoria Hernandez de Alba, head of the Indian commission in Colombia. Dr. Hernandez had read an article by a Colombian anthropologist on the Yuko Indians, so he questioned me about their culture. What I said checked out, of course.

"Okay," he said. "I believe you. You've been with the Yukos."

"But what about the Motilones?" I asked. "You don't believe I've been with them?"

He shrugged and grinned. "No one has ever contacted the Motilones before, so there's no way to check your story."

He put out his hand. "Still, that doesn't matter. I believe you."

He took legal responsibility for me, so that I could get official papers to stay in Colombia. He also gave me money and helped me find a boarding house in which to stay.

A few days later I met an American couple, the Martins, at a Baptist church in Bogota. They invited me to stay with them, gave me money for clothes and other necessities, and introduced me to many of their friends.

I spent most of my time just walking around Bogota. Every day I felt better. It was great to be able to communicate freely. I felt at home, and the more I thought about it the less I wanted to go back to the Motilones. Life was hard in the jungle. I'd spent nearly two years there, sick most of the time, eating terrible food when I ate at all, unable to communicate well: Why should I go back? What was there to draw me back?

Well, I thought, *I'm supposed to be telling the Indians about Jesus. That's what God sent me here to do.*

How was I going to do that? I wasn't about to go back into the jungles and convert them into Americans, like some of the missionaries seemed to do. And with all the Indian myths and stories, legends and strange rites, where was Jesus Christ ever going to have an appeal?

But a man does not desert his wife because it's troublesome to feed her. As much as I wanted to stay away from the jungle, I knew I was going to go back. I *had* to go back. That was where God wanted me. He'd affirmed that too many times to doubt it. And, more important, He'd given me a love for the Motilones that, in view of what I'd been through while I was with them, was unbelievable. I knew that it didn't make sense, but when I was asked about my adventures I found myself more and more describing the Motilone people and the way they lived, and spending less and less time telling what had happened to me. I loved those people. I was proud of them.

However, Bogota was appealing. I loved being there. I wanted to stay as long as I could.

"All right, Lord, I'll go back," I said. "But I don't have any way to get there. When You want me to go back, You open up a way of getting me there."

The people I was staying with, the Martins, worked for Texaco Oil. They were quite interested in my story, and Mr. Martin wanted me to tell it to the general manager of the Colombian Petroleum Company, which is jointly owned by Texaco and Mobil. I agreed to do it, since the Martins had been so kind to me.

Frank Lerory, the general manager, listened attentively to my story. When I finished, he leaned back in his chair and frowned, as if he were going to give me bad news.

"Mr. Olson, we have hired two excellent anthropologists to contact what is known as the Motilone tribe. As you've no doubt heard, it's supposed to be the Motilone Indians who attack our employees.

"The anthropologists, however, on both occasions made contact with the Yuko Indians, and affirmed that these were the people known as the Motilones." He shrugged and put up his hands. "Why should we accept what you're saying?"

I mentioned some of the differences between the way the Motilones and the Yukos live.

"Oh, well," he said, "I suppose you've flown over the area in a plane. Anyone can do that."

That made me angry. "I'm not interested in whether you believe me or not," I said. "I just came in because Mr. Martin asked me to."

He looked bored. "So what do you hope to get from us?"

"I don't want a thing from you," I said. "I just came in at the request of a friend."

He waved his hand. "Okay, you came. Thanks a lot."

I got up and started out of his office without stopping to shake his hand.

"Wait a second," he said. "Do you want to go back to Motilone territory?"

I turned. Immediately I thought of what I had prayed only a few days before.

"Yes," I said, shortly.

"We have a DC-3 going to the River of Gold the day after tomorrow," he said. "I think I can get you on it if you'd like. That's as close as you can get to their territory."

I nodded slowly. "Thank you. I know it is. I would like very much to go."

12

An Impatient Wait

The jungle seemed strangely quiet and serene after a month in Bogota. I established a camp near the bank of a small stream, and waited for the Motilones to find me. The camp was near the juncture of three different Motilone trails, and I knew that I wasn't far from a Motilone home. But it would have been dangerous to go walking up to it. Instead, I left gifts on the trails for the Motilones to find.

My supplies were luxurious compared to my previous jungle equipment. I had a plastic tarp to keep off the night rain, and enough food to last me a week or more. I even had three books: a Bible, *Dr. Zhivago* and *Red Cloth Green Jungle,* an anthropological adventure with the Yuko Indians. I was quite pleased with myself. Soon I would be back with the Motilones, I thought. In the meantime I could enjoy the jungle, do some reading, and rest.

Civilization was far behind me. From the River of Gold,

where the oil company's territory ended, a farmer had guided me upriver as far as he dared. Then I had walked back into the jungle, repeatedly losing my way, back-tracking, and trying to make sense out of the indistinct, tangled Indian trails. Finally I had settled on my camping place.

Every day I checked the gifts I had laid out on the trails. I had draped a long piece of red cloth across branches on one trail, tied small bags of sugar and salt to trees, and left three machetes lying flat on another trail. They lay flat because the Motilones declared war, I had been told by one of the oil company employees, by sticking their arrows point down in the trail. I wanted no confusion: I came in peace.

Checking on the gifts took a good part of each day, since it required fighting through the branches and vines that covered the trails. After doing that I would return to my camp. It was on a knoll, underneath a mahogany tree whose roots jutted out like the flying buttresses of a cathedral. It was a comfortable place, except for the bugs. I usually fished in the afternoon, cooked some food on the fire I kept going, then read.

A week went by, then two weeks. There was no sign that the gifts had been touched. The weeks stretched into a month. My food was gone. The jungle began to seem oppressive. The scream of animals often kept me awake at night. I knew that there were tigers stalking prey out in the dark. Sometimes, hearing an animal scream, I would shiver. During the day the high trees dripped water and looked dark and somber. I wished I could see the sun through the jungle growth. There was a frightening sense of quietness, as though my approach made all the jungle hush up; as though any spoken word would echo endlessly in the stillness. Sometimes, to relieve the silence, I would stand and yell phrases in all the languages I could think of.

I began to doubt whether my gifts would ever get results. Each day when I rounded a corner on the trail I expected to see some change. Each day they were just the way I had left them. I grew impatient. I would—after struggling several hours to get to the gifts—merely glance at them with disgust and leave. I had read my books over and over, and was tired of them. I wanted something to happen.

My impatience seemed ridiculous. Here I had committed my whole life to the Motilones, and I couldn't stand a few weeks waiting comfortably in the jungle. What was the hurry?

All such rational considerations aside, however, I was ecstatically happy when, after two months, I found that my gifts were gone. I could hardly believe it. I checked to see that it was really the same place. But there was no doubting it; I knew the location as well as I knew my hand. I could describe every branch of every tree. The gifts had been taken.

I put out more gifts. The next day they were gone too. Again I set out gifts. That day they were replaced by a bow and arrow. That was a great step forward: they were willing to exchange gifts.

This time I decided to put out gifts and stay nearby, to see if they would take them from me personally. I felt sure that there were eyes in the jungle watching me. I wanted to see them.

So I sat down on the trail and waited. Hours went by. I saw and heard nothing. I had my fishing equipment with me, and there was a stream nearby, so I decided to fish. I probably would hear them if they came to take the gifts.

When I got back from fishing, the gifts were gone. In their place were four long arrows stuck into the ground, point down.

It was the Motilone warning. I should run for my life. But if I ran now I probably would never see them again. My months and years would be wasted. My commitment would be an empty phase of my life.

I got down on my knees and prayed. It seemed the only logical thing to do. When I stood up, I got an idea. I pulled the arrows out of the ground, one by one, and lay them flat. Then I took some gifts and lay them on top. Perhaps that would convince them that I came in peace.

I started walking back to my camp along the trail. As I went I found more symbols. There was a white shirt, cut out and torn to shreds. Farther along the trail I found a manioc root, cut open, with dirt rubbed inside.

What did these things mean? Would the Motilones cut my body open and rub dirt inside? Would they cut me up in ribbons?

I heard a rustling in the underbrush. I stopped and listened. The rustling stopped too.

It's my imagination, I thought. I started walking again. But there were definite sounds near the trail. I was being followed.

I searched the thick, green vegetation with my eyes. I could see nothing. I continued to walk, looking around me constantly, expecting to feel an arrow sizzle into my back.

I remembered a Motilone phrase I had learned while I was with them before. I was fairly sure that it meant, "Come here." I yelled it at the Indians.

"Guaycaba dobucubi! Guaycabo dobucubi!"

After I shouted several times, I heard the rustling noises again, this time retreating from me, back into the jungle. Then there was silence.

Later I learned that "dobucubi" means, "you lazy ones of no value," so that I was yelling, "Come here, you lazy, worthless people!" But I didn't know that then. I didn't know what I had done. Two months of waiting had been turned into nothing by a stupid mistake that I couldn't even identify. I felt horribly frustrated. My hopes, that had been so high that morning, disappeared. I began to run on the trail, back to my camp, slashing through thorn-bushes and vines. All I wanted to do was to get out of that place. I had had it with the Indians. They were stupid and irrational.

So I ran, panting furiously, but not even feeling the fatigue. All the loneliness of the past two months came out. I felt the bushes tear my hands and face, but it almost felt good. I wanted to leave, to forget the Indians.

I broke into the clearing of my camp, and stood panting for a moment. Then I seized my axe and ran down to the water. I began to chop at a balsa-wood tree. I would make a raft and float out of there.

I worked at a frenzy. Soon the tree swayed and came crashing down into the river. Immediately I moved to a second, driving the axebite deep into the tree. It too fell. I moved to a third.

Then I looked up. There were the Motilones—six of them, their bow strings taut. Without thinking I dropped my axe and hid behind a tree. I peered out at them. They didn't seem to have any inclination to kill me. They were just waiting, holding their bows ready.

I stepped out from behind the tree. I held out my hands, showing that they were empty. My anger was gone. I watched their faces for some sign, my hands shaking slightly.

Slowly they relaxed their bows. One of them stepped forward. He was pigeon-toed. I looked more closely at his face. He had a small scar on the side of the mouth.

I smiled at him, hoping that he'd recognize me. He returned my smile. I smiled more broadly. So did he. He knew me. He spoke a word to the other men. They relaxed. Then he broke into the big, long laugh that I had known him for on the other side of the mountains. He had been the only friendly person there, and now I found him here, hundreds of miles away.

The men began talking to each other. They weren't angry, I could tell. They didn't even seem to watch me too closely. Then the man with the laugh motioned to me to follow them, and we set off. This time there were no spears in my back.

When we reached the communal home, I caused a great commotion. Motilones crowded around me, poking, rubbing. They seemed most interested in the hair on my arms and legs. I had noticed before that Motilones didn't have any. One young fellow touched my arm, then took some of the thick blond hair between his fingers and pulled it out.

"Ouch!" I said. The pain was excruciating. But he just laughed, and all the others laughed with him. They pulled on my shirt and shorts, as though they weren't sure whether they were part of my body. They punched me, and kneaded my muscles.

More of my hair was pulled out. It hurt, but they obviously were having a good time. Soon I had to laugh myself. I was exhilarated. They weren't going to hurt me. I had made contact again. Once again I had an opportunity to reach the Motilones.

That night I was given food, then a hammock in which to sleep. The hammock hung so high in the rafters that it took several tries to get up in it. The first time I tried, I fell, and everyone laughed. But I made it up and, feeling a little insecure, tried to relax. The hammock swayed slightly.

Looking at the ceiling I studied the familiar curved rafters. Then I saw what looked like a small mouse coming down one of the hammock ropes toward me. It had an odd, flat shape for an animal. When it ran to within an arm's length, I saw that it was a huge cockroach, perhaps five inches long. I gave a little shriek and knocked it onto the ground. No one seemed to notice. I lay back in the hammock and laughed nervously.

The house became quiet. I heard only an occasional fragment of the sing-song, explosive language of the Motilones.

Soon, I thought, *I'll understand that.*

Yukos

Motilone House Construction

Yukos

House Constructio

Motilone Home

Fishing and Dam Building

Motilone Activities

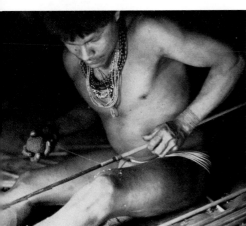

Motilone Activities

Caymiyocba

Bobarishora

Motilone Personalities

Bobarishora

13

Discouragement

The next day we traded names. I pointed at myself. "Bruce Olson," I enunciated clearly.

Most of the people around me looked confused. One of the men tried to say it. "Bruchalonga."

I shook my head. "Bruce Olson. Bruuuce Ohhl-sun." He tried again. "Bruchko."

"Bruce Olson," I said.

He smiled and nodded. "Bruchko", he said. He turned and happily told it to one of the other men near him. "Bruchko." The fellow repeated it tentatively. "Bruchko." Soon the entire group had spread it around. "Bruchko," they repeated, pointing at me.

So I was Bruchko.

I also was a celebrity. They mimicked my speech, squeezed my arms, and/or rubbed my stomach. Sometimes when I was in my hammock, two or three children would climb in with me, jabbering away and crawling over me as though I were a large piece of statuary.

121

I got plenty of good smoked fish and boiled manioc root. It was delicious. The man who had first recognized me, whose name was Arabadoyca, usually brought it to me in a big banana leaf. I would get out of my hammock and eat while he stood, grinning along with the usual crowd of other curious onlookers. Everything I did seemed to interest them. And they were always laughing, singing, or talking.

In the early morning the men would go out hunting, and the women would begin their work for the day. The children would play tag, or would make little arrows and shoot them at targets. Later the men would come back with their kill and there would be a meal, with everyone enjoying the aroma of the roasting meat, shouting back and forth across the center of the community home. Each family cooked its own food, and ate it with obvious pleasure. When they were full, their stomachs bulged, and they would walk around patting each other's almost like proud mothers comparing babies.

Everyone seemed to have taken a liking to me, and I was excited. Already I was working hard to learn the Motilone language, but I could see that it would be a long, slow process.

In Minnesota I had worked with a boys club, and I'd mastered a little act of removing my eye and cleaning it off. Several little boys were in my hammock with me when I thought of the trick. I picked each one up, set him on the ground, and prepared to do my act. Several other children came up to watch.

I put my fingers around one eye and twisted them back and forth, making a grinding sound with my teeth. Then, closing my eye, I pretended to take it out of the socket, breathe on it, then polish it on my shirt. I put it back up to my eye socket, twisted it around a little to get it back into place, and then opened it. Ah! That was much better. I could see much more clearly.

The children loved it. They wanted me to do it with the other eye. So I did. Then I pretended to take both eyes out. In putting them back, I crossed my hands. When I opened my eyes, they were crossed! That was a great sensation.

Most of the children ran off to get other children or to get their parents, so that everyone could see this wonderful performance.

I was pleased at being so well received. But as the people were gathering, I realized that this act might have some practical significance in learning the language. So I reached up to the shelf that ran around the inside of the home and got down a notebook and pencil. While I was doing my act I listened to what the people said, and copied it down as well as I could.

When I took both eyes out, the kids said something like, "Now he will put them in cross-eyed," and I got the future tense.

When I put one of the eyes in my mouth, and, gulp, swallowed it, there was an expression of surprise. "He swallowed it!" one of the little boys gasped. That gave me the past tense.

When I burped the eye back up, I got a past tense that has continuing significance in the present.

I gave the presentation for every Motilone in the home dozens of times, until it seemed that my eyes would turn black and blue. But I was filling my notebook with Motilone words.

Other games that I remembered were helpful, too. I would chop at my arm above the shirt sleeve with my hand, then pull my arm out of the sleeve as though it had broken off. The Motilones would laugh, then chop at their own arms and pull. Nothing would happen. They'd look perplexed, and I'd say, "Why don't you let me do it to you?" They'd laugh and say, "No, you'd break our arms," and run away from me.

Or I would tense my arm and swing it in a circle, as though it had been broken at the elbow and was hanging loose. Of course the Motilones were mystified, because they didn't know the trick.

They had unbelievable tolerance for seeing these acts again and again. But everyone gets tired of games. After a few weeks most of the Motilones lost interest in them, and I did too.

I tried to interest myself more in the adult life of the

home. I watched Arabadoyca make arrows one day—even tried to make one of my own. I did it all wrong, of course, but Arabadoyca was a patient teacher. It was interesting, but took a great deal of practice. After a few days I looked for something else to do.

I began to watch the women weave. Ordinarily they would never let a man sit and observe, but since I was an outsider they put up with me, though they giggled and blushed while I was there. Weaving was an old hobby of mine, and I got quite engrossed in watching them spin thread from the wild cotton they had picked, then weave it into a rough cloth for their skirts. It was a social time for them, and there was lots of conversation to listen to. Of course, I didn't understand any of it, but just getting used to the sounds of the language would help me, I thought. I began to wish that I had a loom of my own to work with. But I knew it wasn't a good idea. If I spent time weaving, the men soon would be put off, since that was women's work.

Like making arrows, watching weaving is interesting for a day, two days, even three days. But after that you can't stand it any more.

I began to wish that the day would last about three hours, and that the rest of the time would be filled with sleep. I would lie up in my hammock for hours at a time during the day, staring at the high ceiling, wishing that I would fall asleep. I started going to bed early, immediately after eating the evening meal. But then I would wake up at two in the morning so I made myself stay awake at night. I would stare at something or try to make myself listen to someone's meaningless talking, until it was late enough to go to bed.

A fog of depression began to cover my days. It seemed that the sun didn't move across the sky at all, that each day lasted forever, and that it was like every other day.

I shouldn't have been unhappy. The Motilones were a cheerful, gentle people. One day I watched a mother weaving with her little girl in her lap. The girl put her hands into the cloth and tangled the thread until it was a complete mess. But the mother didn't even scold her. She merely put her to one side, patiently repaired the damage, then showed her how she could help card the yarn.

And once I saw two brothers fighting. Their mother, upset, picked up a chicken's head and gently pecked at one of the boy's legs. She hardly touched him, but the boy broke into tears because he had grieved his mother. That was the strongest form of punishment I ever saw used, or needed.

But there were things that I was not so attracted to. The communal home, housing approximately eighty Motilones, should have been a perfect place for cooperative living. But each family lived a life of its own. If one family happened to have too much food on a particular day, they would throw it away, regardless of whether the family next to them was starving or not. There were no close ties between families. One family might live next to another for some time without even exchanging names.

And the population of the home changed constantly. A family would just get up and leave, without warning. Other days families would appear, and settle down with us, without anyone taking much notice of them or seeming to care whether they came or not. Often weeks would go by before anyone even knew who they were.

No tears were ever shed, no sign of pain or sadness ever shown. The Motilones didn't seem to have those emotions. The smiles and constant laughing began to seem pointless.

When you get right down to it, these are uncivilized Indians, with none of the feelings I can relate to, I thought.

I had read my Bible through again and again, until it too seemed almost stale. I knew what verses were coming next. I knew the thoughts I'd thought about those passages, and the prayers I'd prayed. True, there was clear evidence that God had heard those prayers. After all I was there, living peacefully with the notorious Motilone Indians.

But the excitement was gone. I had come to communicate Jesus Christ to the Motilone Indians. Was I doing that? I didn't know the language beyond a few rudimentary phrases.

I thought about some of the great missionaries whose

biographies I had read. Nothing about them seemed to help my situation. Great obstacles I could face, but what could I do about the terrible, flat boredom? I started thinking about missionaries like the ones I had met in Minneapolis, and the missionaries I had become so critical of who worked on the Orinoco. After four years they got to go home on furlough and tell about their converts.

It was that silly thought that started me feeling really low. I had been in South America for three years. Where were my converts? There were my friends at the University of course, but I couldn't think of them as converts. They were just friends with whom I'd had an opportunity to share.

And after three years, I had no money, no mission board to buy my ticket home. In fact, the only place in the world where I was sure of getting something to eat was in the jungle, with the Motilones.

So I became discouraged. Each morning I dreaded the thought of eating. The food had grown as dull, or duller than the Yuko food. With no salt or sugar, there was a limit to how good it could taste. And often, when there was only monkey meat or grub worms, I would vomit it all up. My fleas were getting worse, and I had a skin rash from being constantly dirty.

And why was the language so hard? I had thought I was making progress the first few days, but it seemed now that it was harder than learning Yuko. I didn't want to spend three months completely without communication, as I had with the Yukos. I was always looking for shortcuts, but there were none.

One morning, completely disgusted with the endless store of time on my hands, I got out of my hammock and went outside. As I ducked out of the door, I slipped and almost fell. I had stepped on a pile of human manure. I scraped it off my shoe as well as I could then walked over to a stump and sat down. It was about eleven o'clock. The sun was coming almost straight down, making it hot and steamy. There were no trees near the home for shade or comfort. Flies buzzed in the sun over other piles of excrement.

Why did they have to do it right outside the door? Couldn't they go somewhere else to do it, where it wouldn't bother anyone?

Just then one of the wives came to the door and threw out a bunch of garbage: banana and pineapple peels and all sorts of thing left over from the fish and monkeys we had eaten.

By their standards, of course, she'd been hygienic. One woman hadn't thrown out her garbage for a week. It had laid on the floor until toadstools grew on it.

What a filthy place! My chest felt tight. I closed my eyes to make it all go away.

An old lady came out of the house and walked over to me, grinning a big toothless grin. She rubbed up against me in a friendly way, jabbering. She smelled bad. I looked at her tangled, thick black hair. Lice were crawling through it. Her breasts hung down flabbily.

I stood up and walked from her, feeling sick. She followed, put her hands around my waist and hugged me. Then she laughed—a stupid, lunatic laugh. I looked down at her hands. They were filthy. I gingerly took each one off me, and walked a little way into the jungle. She followed at a distance, giggling.

I couldn't even tell her to get lost. A simple thing like that, and I couldn't say it. There wasn't a soul there who understood me.

How long would it take? Three months? Four? Would I be able to communicate well in a year?

There's an old gospel song that says, "If you can't bear the cross, then you can't wear the crown." I realized I didn't want the cross. I wanted the crown, with all its jewels, without ever carrying the cross.

Looking again at the old woman, I wasn't even sure I wanted the crown.

14

A Pact Brother

I lay in my hammock, watching the cockroaches crawl across the ceiling. What was I going to do today? Would I be able to contribute anything . . . do anything at all to help these people?

A boy brought me some food. I eased down out of the hammock. I didn't feel like eating.

The boy looked at me with a big smile—a sweet smile—and I realized I'd seen him before. In fact, he often was assigned to bring me food.

I squatted down to eat, and he lingered. I motioned to him to sit down, and he did. Dark and muscular, he appeared to be about thirteen, for he did not yet have the G-string that is the sign of a Motilone man.

I offered him some food, but he refused.

"What is your name?" I asked.

"Cobaydra," he said.

That was about as far as my vocabulary would take me. I had been with the Motilones for nearly a year. We sat and looked at each other while I ate. The entire time he wore that smile. I almost wanted to throw my arms around him and hug him.

It was the day for a Motilone fishing expedition. I had never gone along on one, but this time, as the men and women were leaving the home, Cobaydra came and took me by the arm. "Come on," he said.

It was about four miles to the river. By the time I got there I was tired. The river was broad and shallow, divided in the middle by a long sandbar. It was a hot day, and a swim would feel good. Besides I was dirty! But no one stopped. The men went upstream, and the women downstream. I hesitated, then followed the men. They were already out of sight. I fought through brambles to get to where I could hear them shouting. When I saw them again, they already were carrying huge rocks out into the stream, beginning a dam.

I thought I would help, so I stepped into the stream and tried to pull up a rock that looked about the size of the ones they were carrying. I couldn't budge it. I strained and pushed, but couldn't move it from its place.

Well, I thought, *this must be heavier than the rocks they're lifting.*

As I looked around for a smaller one, I jumped: standing right behind me, with the same sweet smile, was Cobaydra. He walked past me, easily lifted the rock, carried it over, and put it in place. I was chagrined, but he smiled at me, flexed his muscles, and laughed. I laughed too. We began to work together.

It took most of the morning to build the dam. When all the rocks were in place we got big leaves from the trees and covered the rocks with them. That diverted the water to the other side of the sandbar. Meanwhile, downstream, the women had been building a small dam to keep the fish from swimming downriver.

Then brandishing long, pencil-thin spears, the men dashed up and down the river, aiming inerrantly at the fish. They yelled and laughed, charging through the water, and coming out with huge fish wriggling at the end of their spears. I sat on the bank, watching—and drying off.

Cobaydra came over and offered me his spear. He wanted me to try.

I shook my head, *No.*

Cobaydra nodded his head, *Yes.* His smile was beguiling. I couldn't refuse him.

He followed me into the water which was now thick and brown from all the splashing. I couldn't see a fish anywhere.

Cobaydra grabbed my arm, and pointed into the stream. I looked but saw nothing. He kept pointing. Finally I spotted the fish. Carefully I raised my spear, aimed, and let fly. The spear went off balance and glanced sideways into the water, making a splash but missing the fish. Disgusted, I retrieved the spear and handed it to Cobaydra. Still smiling, he handed it back.

"Take it," he said. "Try it again."

I had a friend. From that day on, things went better. Cobaydra brought my food almost every day, and I looked forward to sitting with him and eating. He made me go with him when the men went hunting, so I had more to do. I also became familiar with the projects and pastimes of the men. Hunting was fun, particularly with Cobaydra to run the trails with me.

I wanted to show Cobaydra and the rest of the men that I really was interested in hunting. I couldn't tell them directly, because I didn't know the right words. So I made a great show of shouting when they did, following after them and mimicking their phrases.

One morning I had a sore throat from yelling. I could hardly talk at first. Later, my voice was lower than usual. That afternoon I got hungry, went to Cobaydra, and asked for a banana. He went out and came back with an axe. I was puzzled. I was sure I had the right word for banana. So I asked for it again, and again Cobaydra handed me the axe.

Then a crazy thought came into my head. I pinched my nose and asked again in a high voice. This time Cobaydra got me a banana.

The Motilones had a tonal language! According to all the linguistic books, tonal languages did not exist in South America. Now I was trying to learn one, and without my flute I couldn't even carry a tune. How would I ever manage?

But in Cobaydra I had someone I could talk to without feeling embarrassed. We spent hours lying in hammocks or squatting inside the house. I wrote down the things he said, and gradually my store of words increased.

Cobaydra's father was a distinguished member of the tribe. He was the only Motilone with white hair. Sensitive to our friendship, he encouraged us to spend time together.

He came up to me one day and told me to follow him. We went outside. Cobaydra was waiting there, looking nervous.

Two other Motilone men were with him. They walked into the jungle, without exchanging a word. I followed. What was going on? We walked for about fifteen minutes, then stopped in a little clearing.

Cobaydra's father solemnly produced a G-string, and I realized with a little chill of excitement that this was the ceremony for Cobaydra to become a man. I had no idea what took place. All I knew was that one day a Motilone boy was a boy, and the next day he was wearing a G-string and was considered a man.

There was a short ceremony, then Cobaydra slipped on the G-string. He was smiling, almost laughing . . . and really proud.

His father turned to the three of us who were looking on. "His name is Bobarishora." Then, turning to me, he said, "Now that he is a man, he will no longer be called Cobaydra. He will be called Bobarishora."

Trying to repeat the name, I got it all tangled up on my tongue.

"Bobarishora," his father said again, slowly.

I looked at Bobarishora. He was smiling. I tried the name again. "Bobbishow." That's the way it sounded to me. "Bobbishow." Then I shortened it.

"Bobby," I said and laughed. The name seemed to fit his pleasant light-hearted personality.

The others repeated it. They liked it, and later the whole tribe adopted it. Bobarishora became known as Bobby, though Bobarishora was still his full name.

Being invited to Bobby's initiation ceremony was significant, because only the closest family and friends ever were allowed to observe the rites. However I knew enough of the Motilone culture to realize that something was missing. Usually a pact was established with anyone invited. In my case there was none.

The Motilone social system is based upon pacts between families. If you form a pact with someone you agree to share everything: food, shelter and family. But it goes even deeper than that. You become brothers.

I had seen pacts formed before. Part of the ceremony required that the people involved exchange arrows. I wanted to establish a pact with Bobby, and I felt that he wanted it, too. But I couldn't make arrows well enough, and the exchange of the arrows was an important beginning of the whole relationship.

I asked Bobby's brother to make some arrows for me, and to arrange the pact. As the time for the pact ceremony approached, I actually became quite nervous. I wanted very much for Bobby to be pleased with it, and I was afraid of making a mistake.

But it went well. I held out my arrows to Bobby, and he took them and made a show of carefully examining them.

"These are beautiful arrows," he said solemnly. "I accept you as my brother."

I took his arrows from him. They were long, heavy things, with beautiful markings. I could see that Bobby, who had been making arrows all his life, had taken extra care with these.

We sang the traditional song of brotherhood, and my body relaxed. "We are brothers," I sang, looking at Bobby, my face breaking out into a smile that was as broad and free as his. "We are brothers, and there is nothing in the world that can take us apart."

More and more of our time was spent together. When I went out of the communal home to walk the Motilone trails, Bobby followed me without a word. That had deep significance. It meant that he was accepting me as his leader, as his personal chieftain. Often we went hunting together. One day I stepped on a five-inch jungle thorn. As I pulled my foot out of my tennis shoe, blood spurted everywhere. Bobby ran around and around, making little crying noises, until I could stop screaming and get the blood stopped. Motilones never show pain, yet Bobby had given me sympathy and had wanted to help.

A few weeks later when we were walking in the jungle Bobby stopped behind me without saying a word. For a moment I didn't realize that he had stopped, because he walked so quietly. When I did, I turned around. He looked a little shaky, and his mouth was open as if he were trying to speak.

"Bobby," I said, "what's the matter?"

"Nothing," he said in a low mutter. I shrugged and turned back to the trail. We kept on, neither of us talking. The silence was unnerving. I wondered what was wrong.

Then I heard his voice behind me. "Bruchko, I am named, 'In the Heavens.' "

I turned, puzzled. He was standing quite still, with his mouth open a little bit, as if he'd seen a ghost. I could see that whatever he meant was extremely important. But I didn't understand.

"That's my name," he said.

"But what about Bobarishora?"

He shook his head. "No, my real name is 'In the Heavens.' That is my secret name."

Then he explained that every Motilone Indian has a secret name that is his real identity. Only his father and sometimes a few others know it. It is secret because, if someone knows it, he has complete power over that person.

"And you are telling me?" I asked. "You are telling me your secret name, and giving me power over your life?"

He nodded. We stood looking at each other. It was one of the most serious moments of my life.

Then Bobby's face broke into a smile again. I reached out and took him by the shoulders. I was crying. I had come all the way to South America, to Colombia, and now to the jungle, needing something I hadn't really expected to find: a real friend. Someone who would be a brother. A blood brother. I had found him. Our ages were different, our language, our skin color, our beliefs, everything. But we had one thing together: a deep, brother love. I didn't know where it would take us. But God had placed it in our hearts.

15
Mistaken for a Cannibal

After Bobby and I became brothers, the dirt was still there, the fleas still bit, the bugs still carried disease, and I still got diarrhea. But those things seemed less and less significant.

I had been accepted. I had a family.

Bobby and I began to visit in the various communal homes. Our times on the trail were great! The jungle seemed even more beautiful as Bobby and I walked, talked and sang together.

The Motilone communal homes are spread over a wide area. It sometimes took several days to get from one home to another. Bobby was one of the strongest young Motilone warriors, and his pace on the trails was far too fast for me. When he noticed I was exhausted he stopped without a word and we rested.

But he was proud. He wouldn't accept anything from anyone. When we arrived at a communal home, he sometimes would wait days before accepting food. To eat was a sign of weakness, and no weakness could be tolerated.

"Bobby, why don't you eat?" I would ask.

"I'm not hungry," he would reply.

Bobby was so determined to be stronger than anyone else that he wasn't always popular with other Motilones. He was merciless with himself. But with me he was kind and gentle.

We came back from one trip to find that Bobby's father had died. Bobby told me, showing no emotion. I was hurt and puzzled. He had been such a fine old man. He had taken me into his own family. He had encouraged my friendship with Bobby. Now he was dead. He had died during the night. His body was still in his hammock.

No one seemed to care. It was the first Motilone funeral I had ever seen, and I couldn't believe how callous everyone was. His body was wrapped in his hammock and taken by a few men out to the jungle. It was hung high up in the trees. Soon the vultures came swinging down out of the sky to devour it.

There were no tears. It seemed as though nothing had happened. I wrote in my journal, "These people are iron hard. To them the death has no great significance. They aren't struck by any spiritual dimension at all. The fact that he will not walk the face of the earth again seems to have no impact on their lives. And how will I reach them with Jesus' message of love if they don't even try to love each other?"

Everywhere I went in Motilone territory I heard the name Abaratatura. It always was spoken with awe and respect. In the Motilone language, the name has a special lilt that gives it an almost magical quality. Finally I asked Bobby who he was.

Bobby wrinkled his forehead. "He is a great warrior and hunter, highly respected by all the Motilones. I suppose you could say that he's a chief over the chiefs."

"Where does he live?"

"In Corroroncayra. That's a long way from here, in the mountains."

"Bobby, why don't we visit him? I'd like to meet him."

Bobby laughed, and shook his head. "You want to get

killed? He hates white men."

The thought of it was rather chilling. I had almost forgotten that the Motilones killed people; that I might have enemies.

I was talking to Arabadoyca one day, lying in our hammocks, and it popped into my head to ask him about Abaratatura. "Why would he want to kill me? He must know by now that I'm not dangerous. Surely he's heard about me living here."

"He thinks you're the cannibal with the magic flute," Arabadoyca said. "So he'll kill you before you kill him."

"What?" I said. "What do you mean?"

Arabadoyca stretched. "The time will come, it's said, when a white man will come to the Motilones with a magic flute that he will play. He'll lead all the Motilones into a trap, and they'll be eaten alive."

I knew that the Motilones had extensive traditions, but I had heard only a few of them. This one was new to me.

"And that's why Abaratatura hates me? He thinks I'm a cannibal?"

"Well, you play the flute, don't you?" He laughed. "Anyway, the rest of us don't think you are the cannibal. At first we thought you were. In fact, Abaratatura was on his way to kill you when you disappeared the first time you came to us. The day after you left, he arrived."

I remembered the night when, sick, I had slipped out of the house, wondering what on earth I was doing. Now I could see that God had given me that compulsion, to save my life.

"When no harm came to us because of you," Arabadoyca continued, "most of us believed that you were all right. In fact, some thought that you might be bringing God's banana stalk."

"What's that?"

"There is another prediction that a tall man with yellow hair will come with a banana stalk, and God will come out of the banana stalk."

"And do you think that might be me?"

He shrugged. "You don't carry a banana stalk, do you?"

"Well," I said, "what about Abaratatura? I would like to see him."

Arabadoyca shook his head. "You can't go there. He'll kill you."

Once I had the idea in my head, though, I couldn't get it out. A few weeks later a contingent of men were going up to call on Abaratatura, and I asked to go with them. I was turned down, but I insisted. Reluctantly they agreed.

It was a long trip. We set a fierce pace, not stopping to eat. We lived on raw manioc roots, lizards, and beetles. After eight days I had shooting pains in my chest, and began to vomit every time I tried to eat. My mouth felt as though it were filled with cotton. At every stream I drank water until my stomach felt ready to burst, but still my mouth had no saliva in it. That ninth day stretched out interminably. Finally, when there were still hours of walking left, I had to ask my companions to stop for the day.

I tried to eat some of the food that Arabadoyca brought me, but it wouldn't stay down. I couldn't imagine what this sickness could be. My mind went over my medical books, trying to match my symptoms.

Arabadoyca came up and took me by the shoulders. His crooked smile seemed stretched and far away, like a figure in a dream.

"Bruchko," he said, "your eyes are beautiful! How did you make them such a pretty color?"

It took me a moment to comprehend what he was saying. His face seemed to sway before me. "What color?" I asked.

"Why, they're yellow, a beautiful yellow. Can we make our eyes like that, too?"

Yellow eyes. Hepatitis! I needed more than rest. I needed medical attention.

But it was eight days back to the river, then another week to make a raft and float downriver to civilization. I wouldn't make it alive.

But could I go on? I wouldn't be any closer to help in Corroroncayra. And there I faced the possibility of being killed outright. I certainly didn't have the strength to fight.

Either way there was no hope. The trunks of the jungle trees seemed to swing back and forth in front of me. I was sick, and now, I thought, with my stomach sinking, I am going to die.

I remembered the promise I had made God when I was a captive of the Yukos. I had promised to lead a God-directed life. What was His direction now?

I decided I had to go on. My life was in God's hands. He would have to do with it what He wanted.

The next few days were trance-like. My skin turned dark yellow. Each step was a struggle. I would feel my body reel and fight to keep balance. Once I fainted and woke up lying on the trail, with Motilone faces surrounding me. I got to my feet and kept walking.

A few hours later I fainted again. When I woke up, one of the men—a witch doctor—was howling and chanting over me. I was frightened, but too weak to move. His face came closer. It seemed huge and inhuman. He took a knife and cut my forehead. I could feel the blood dribbling across my face, but I couldn't move to stop him.

He took a gourd, spilled out a light powder and rubbed it into the cut, constantly chanting his incantations.

I lifted my arms over my head, and managed to make him stop. I told them I didn't think the medicine would work on me, since I wasn't a Motilone. I begged them to make him stop. The witch doctor continued to lean over me, and my hands, up over my head, shook while I talked.

They discussed it. The witch doctor wasn't happy with my attitude. But they decided he had better stop, as long as I didn't want to be treated.

Two Motilones took me under their arms and carried me. My legs dragged along the ground. Sometimes I would faint. The trail seemed endless. Day after day we went on, the Motilones taking turns carrying me. I was barely conscious of what was going on. Occasionally I would sit down on the ground, and my body would sprawl itself out, as if it had a mind of its own. Then hands would grasp me at the armpits and I would be pulled up, and begin to bounce along again. It hurt. I would open my mouth to cry and nothing would come out.

At the end of the second week we arrived at Corroroncayra. A few miles from the home, we were met by a little band of men. They had orders to kill me. The chief had learned that I was coming, and he was infuriated.

I heard the discussion, but it seemed far away. I listened to each opinion objectively. I didn't care if I died.

"He's sick," Arabadoyca told them. "You can't kill a sick man. And anyway, he's a good man. He'll do you no harm."

They inspected me. There was no doubt that I was sick. "Okay," one of the men said, "let's take him to Abaratatura."

Once again I was taken by the arms and pulled along the trail, up a hill. At the top of the hill we came into a clearing. I saw the Motilone home. A man came out of one of the doors. "Drop him," he said. "Drop the cannibal!"

It was Abaratatura. Arabadoyca stood between him and me. "You can't kill him," he said. "He is dying."

The Motilones will never shoot any animal or a man who is soon to die a natural death. They think it will put a hex on their arrow that will make it break in flight, and they will starve to death.

The thought stopped Abaratatura. "What do you mean, he is dying?" he said. "He will certainly die when I put an arrow through him."

"And your people will starve to death," Arabadoyca said. "It will put a hex on all their arrows. This man is dying."

Abaratatura walked over to me. He couldn't disagree.

He spat on the ground, looked disgustedly at me, then ordered them to put me in a hammock. He did not speak to me. He had a regal air, and his orders were obeyed instantly.

For two weeks I stayed in his home, I slept hours on end. When I did wake up I prayed to be able to sleep more. Pain seemed to cut into my bones.

I am going to die, I thought. I wasn't scared. It seemed interesting. *I am going to die. I wonder what it will be like.* The thought tumbled over and over in my mind.

One afternoon I woke to a sudden commotion. Children were running, women were screaming. "The flute is coming! The cannibal will eat us!" I heard someone shout.

People streamed out of the doors, pushing against each other, running to hide. Abaratatura picked up his bow and came toward me.

"We should kill the cannibal before the flute arrives for him," he said.

I could hear the sound they were running from. It took me minutes to recognize it. It was the "flub-flub-flub" of a helicopter. What was it doing here?

The noise got closer and louder. Abaratatura hesitated, frightened, but wanting to kill me. Then he ran out the door. Only Arabadoyca was left in the house. His eyes were big, and he looked ready to run too. He thought I had betrayed him.

"Please take me outside," I said. My voice could barely be heard.

He hesitated, then—with great difficulty—lifted me out of the hammock, got me outside, and set me down in the clearing. Then he ran into the jungle.

I saw the helicopter, but couldn't raise my arms to wave for help. I could only hope that a blond head would surprise the pilot enough to bring him down for a closer look.

"Please, God, have him land," I prayed.

The helicopter hovered overhead, swung around, then settled on the clearing, whipping leaves and rubbish aside with its wind. A man got out, and walked over to me.

"Olson," he said. "you look terrible, like a skeleton," It was Dr. Hans Baumgartner, whom I had met with Dr. Christian on our trip up the Orinoco years before.

I could barely smile. He and the pilot carried me onto the helicopter, and headed for a hospital in Tibu.

After I had been in the hospital four days I began to hemorrhage internally. The doctors said that if I had stayed another six hours in the jungle without medicine I would have died.

Dr. Baumgartner and the pilot came to see me.

"You can't imagine what a surprise it was, Olson, to see you. The helicopter belongs to the oil company, you know, and Manuel is the pilot. It wasn't being used the day I was here, so we went out joyriding. We thought we'd take a swing over Motilone territory to see if we could get some pictures.

"Man," he said shaking his head, "can you imagine going to take pictures of a fierce, stone-age tribe and finding a blond-headed American in front of the tribal home?" He laughed. We all did. But I knew that Someone had prompted them to come my way.

My doctor at the hospital was Alfredo Landinez. We became good friends. He was interested in the Motilones— had even written a thesis on the extraction of the Motilone arrow, a thesis which had been presented to the Harvard School of Tropical Medicine.

After I had been in the hospital several weeks I asked Dr. Landinez when I could go back to the jungle.

"You'll be in treatment for another six months," he said. "You've just about destroyed your liver. Then you'll need to spend another year in convalescence."

"What?" I said. "A year and a half before I can go back to the jungle?"

He shook his head. "You'll never be able to go back to the jungle. Your liver is permanently damaged."

I looked at my hands. They were the color of an orange. I was getting blood transfusions because I still was bleeding internally.

"You're wrong," I said. "I'm going back."

"Thataboy," he said, smiling wryly and patting me on the shoulder. "Keep up your attitude."

Three weeks later they released me from the hospital. Dr. Landinez couldn't quite believe that I was well. "Bruce," he said, "please don't go back into the jungle."

I was already preparing to leave. "Why not?" I asked.

"You're not well enough. You could have a relapse and die out there with no one to care for you."

I shook my head and smiled. "I told you, I'm not going to die. God is going to heal my body better than you ever could."

He shrugged.

"Now I have a request to make of you," I said. "You know that I know quite a bit about medicine. I need some drugs to take back to the Indians. They have no care at all. I know it's illegal to give them to me, and I don't have any money to pay for them. But the Motilones need them."

Although he was risking his job and his career to do it, he took a quantity of oil-company drugs and gave them to me.

"What is the value of my job," he asked, "if I'm not helping people? Maybe these will never help anyone. But you don't take chances with medicine. You give it out, and hope it won't be wasted."

A week later I walked back into the jungle. I had a compass, and I knew where I was heading: straight toward the home of Abaratatura.

On the third day I began to feel dizzy. The chest pains had returned. My urine was dark. I fell asleep that night feeling terrible.

"Father," I prayed, "You brought me here to work with the Motilone Indians. I have medicine that can help them. Please, God, heal my body."

The next morning I woke up feeling fine. There was no more pain, and my urine was clear. I got up and continued walking.

When I reached his communal home, Abaratatura met me on the trail. Someone had seen me coming, and had reported it to him.

16

Using the Witch Doctor

I was frightened. Would he try to kill me?

I looked more closely. Abaratatura wasn't carrying any weapons.

"We thought you had died," he said, "and that the vultures had come to take your body. But God has preserved you."

"Yes," I said, "He has indeed."

I stayed at Abaratatura's home. He had concluded that I wasn't going to try to deceive him and his people. As a result, I found acceptance for me on the part of the Motilones. I got word to Bobby, and he came up to be with me.

My brief stay in civilization had convinced me more than ever that I belonged in the jungle. And I had brought back one product of civilization that made life more comfortable: a flea collar. They had been introduced in Colombia shortly before I arrived at the hospital. I noticed one on a dog, and asked Dr. Landinez about it.

"That's a flea collar," he said. "It's the latest thing.
You put it around your dog's neck and it kills all his fleas
for the next six months."

"Great," I said, "I've got to get one of those."

Dr. Landinez looked puzzled. "You have dogs in the
jungle?"

"No, no," I said, and started to laugh. "No, we don't
have dogs, but we sure have fleas!" I laughed again, and
that was the last sensible word he got out of me on the
subject. Now I had one around my neck, and I was doing
a lot less scratching.

My mind, however, was occupied with thoughts of the
medicines I had brought with me. Motilones were constantly dying from disease, and I knew that the medicine
would cure many of them. But the Motilones already had
their own system for curing people, and they had no
reason to believe that mine was better. Several times I
offered my medicines to sick people, but they wouldn't
take them.

"Leave it to the witch doctor," they said. "She knows our
customs and our ways."

And sometimes they got well. Then they'd come around
and smile at me, as though to say. "You see, we are not
as stupid as you think."

But when an epidemic of pinkeye hit them, I had a perfect case, because pink eye is cured easily with antibiotics.
In no time, almost all the Motilones had it, and were going
around scratching their eyes, feeling miserable. The witch
doctor began to sing incantations day in and day out: up
to twenty hours a day. She was tremendously dedicated
to her people.

After a week it was obvious that her incantations weren't
helping. I went over to talk to her. She was lying on a
mat, resting. Her face was lined with fatigue.

"I have a potion called Terramycin," I said. "It will cure
this disease if you put it in the people's eyes."

"I already used potions," she said. "They didn't work."

"But this is a different kind of potion," I said. "It will
work. I have seen it work many times before."

She looked slightly interested. "Where does this potion
come from?"

"It is one that witch doctors of my people use."

Her interest left. She shrugged. "You are white. Your ways are different from ours." She got to her feet, turned her back on me, and began to sing again.

I went for a walk to think it over. Pinkeye itself wasn't dangerous, but the infection could lead to other more serious things. It needed to be cured, and I had the cure.

The only thing I could do was try to convince someone to let me try the medicine on him. Then I would have proof that my methods worked, and those of the witch doctor didn't.

But then I would be in competition with the witch doctor. Either I would destroy her and her role in the tribe, or she would have to get rid of me.

Missionaries, I knew, often had felt that the witch doctor was a demon element, and had to be eliminated. But it didn't seem to be the case here. The Motilone witch doctor didn't pray to demons. She tried to help her people by praying to God in the best way she knew. I didn't want to destroy what she was doing. I wanted to help her.

I got an idea. I strode back to the home and over to a man who had a bad case of the disease. I rubbed my fingers in the corner of his eye, then smeared his pus in my own eye.

In five days I had developed pinkeye. I went to the witch doctor and told her that I needed her help. She sang incantations for me, just as she had for all the others. Naturally, it didn't help me any more than it had them.

So I went to see the witch doctor again. I told her that I wanted her to try putting Terramycin in my eyes while she sang incantations. She looked doubtful, but by then was willing to try something new. She took the tube of Terramycin, smeared some in my eye, and sang her prayers that God would heal me.

In three days my eyes had cleared up and I felt fine. Everyone else, of course, still was miserable. The witch doctor kept singing her chants and prayers.

I waited for the right time to talk to her again. I didn't want to insult her in any way. One evening I saw her walk out of the home, her shoulders stooped with fatigue.

I followed her outside into the dark, and caught her arm. She turned around.

I held up the tube of Terramycin. "Why don't you try this potion?" I said. "You cured my eyes with it. Perhaps it will work with your people as well."

Within three days she had cured everyone. It increased her stature in the home. She was proud of having been effective with her chants and her new potion, and became a good friend of mine—also a channel for other health measures.

Being able to use simple antibiotics through the witch doctor was a giant step toward my goal of helping the Motilones. But there were so many germs in the filth that surrounded the houses, and in the other unsanitary Motilone practices, that more trouble with disease was inevitable. Some would be sure to go beyond the reach of the medicines I had.

"What's the cause of all these sicknesses?" I asked the witch doctor. "There doesn't seem to be any end to them."

She was surprised that I didn't know. "It's the evil spirits showing their power. That's why we use the chants. We call on God to cast the evil spirits out."

"And why doesn't He always do it?" I asked.

Her face fell, and she turned aside. "We have deceived God," she said in a low, sad voice.

I stood behind her, puzzled, feeling as though behind what she said was something I needed to understand.

"How did you deceive God?" I asked.

"A man came who claimed to be a prophet," she said. "He said that he could take us over the horizon, to a land where there was a better hunt. His name was Sacamaydodji. We left God and followed him."

"When did all this happen?" I asked softly.

She said nothing for a moment, then swept her arm out. "Many, many years ago. We have only heard the story. But we know that he has deceived us. We are far away from God."

Later I went to her and told her that I wanted her to see some of the evil spirits that led to disease and death. I took out my microscope and put a lump of dirt under it.

I had her look into the eyepiece.

"Oh, yes, I can see them dancing around," she said and began singing her chants.

Then I put some disinfectant on the dirt, and told her to look again. She saw that the disinfectant had killed the germs. It shook her. She had seen that the germs didn't die when she sang her chants.

Over a period of time, she introduced disinfectants into the normal ceremonies of the Motilones. There was, for instance, a cleansing ceremony when a new communal home was built. All the Motilones who are going to live in the home gather, sing chants, and strike the walls with sticks to make any evil spirits leave. The witch doctor, at my suggestion, had them begin to use disinfectants with the ceremony, and people noticed that health measurably improved. She also had the midwives begin using disinfectants when mothers gave birth, and the mortality rate declined.

Health measures spread to other homes, and I was increasingly thankful for Dr. Landinez's willingness to supply us with medicine. Motilone food also improved because of the introduction of crops. The Motilone people had relied only on hunting and wild plants for their food. Working with Abaratatura, however, I was able to show them how to raise corn and cattle.

In a few years there were eight health stations (one in each home) that gave shots, antibiotics, and other medicines. These stations also were in charge of seeing that the Motilone homes were kept free from germs. Each home developed its own agricultural system as well, and eventually schools were established.

The health centers, the farms, and the schools were not set up or staffed by civilized white people. They were staffed by the primitive Motilone Indians. I was the only outsider in the Motilone area. The shots were given by the Motilones. The correct medicines were chosen by the Motilones.

It is considered by many to be the fastest example of development that has ever occurred in a primitive tribe. How did it happen? How was this possible?

There are two reasons. The first is simple: The Motilones were not asked to give up their own culture and become white men. Everything introduced was built on things they already knew. Vaccination, for instance, was introduced by the witch doctor as a new form of the traditional blood-letting that the Motilones practiced when someone was sick, because, like blood-letting, it gave a pain that overcame the greater pain of disease or death. Explained in that way, and administered by the witch doctor, who was known and trusted, it quickly was accepted, and spread through the tribe as quickly as needles and vaccine could be provided. And because the witch doctors had seen germs, and understood their danger, correct sanitary procedures were followed.

Agriculture wasn't as much a new idea as medicine, but it would not have been accepted if it had opposed the traditional way of doing things. But because Abaratatura and the other chiefs, who traditionally were responsible for providing food, introduced the idea, it was accepted readily, and without the disruptions of society that often go with economic development. There were no revolts against the old way of the elders; it was the elders who introduced the new ways.

But I said there were two reasons. The second was the Holy Spirit. Without Him, there would have been no real or lasting development.

As I mentioned, it seemed that the Motilones did not care for each other in any deep way. Each man was responsible for himself, and his family, and no one else. This was particularly hard for me to accept in Bobby.

I wanted to see that all the tribes got the medicine they needed, and that they knew how to care for the plants that had been introduced. Bobby went with me on my inspection tours. We had delightful hours on the trails, visiting many of the places we had been before. We talked deeply about life, and about what we desired for ourselves and each other. Bobby hoped to be a warrior-leader of the Motilones like Abaratatura. I hoped to help lead the Motilones to the true way. We shared these things, hunted together, and sang together. We could sense each other's feelings without saying a word.

But Bobby didn't share my concern for the other tribal members. At one point, there was serious disease in two widely separated communal homes. They both needed medicine quickly.

"Bobby," I said, "you go to Iquicarora with some medicine, and I'll go up into the highlands. We'll meet again here."

He looked hurt. "I want to go with you, Bruchko."

I frowned. "Bobby, you can't. There just isn't time to go to both places together."

"So let's go to just one place."

Finally Bobby went by himself because I told him to. He wouldn't have done it of his own free will. It hurt me, and I couldn't understand it.

Everyone else shared Bobby's attitude. People would die in one home because the next home wouldn't bother to take them medicine. A cow would die because its keeper was sick, and couldn't care for it, and no one else would. It became more and more of a struggle for me to be everywhere help was needed. Bobby would pitch in if I asked him, but only because of our friendship.

I got tired. I had been with the Motilones four years. Some of the things I had managed to introduce were good. But I had to work to keep them going. I began to question the point of it all. Why should I care if a few Motilones, more or less, got sick? What were their lives worth? To the rest of the world they could die to a man and never be missed.

Yet, as I pondered one day while seated in front of the communal home, I knew that the answer had to be the same as it had been four years before. The significance of Motilone lives, and of what I was doing, wasn't in what people thought. I remembered what God had told me: "Everyone may reject you, but I will not reject you." That had to be true for the Motilones, too. God would not reject them. He loved them. That was why I had come into the jungle: to let them see and experience the love of God.

But I still could not see how to do it. I knew too much about Motilone beliefs. Nothing I could say about Jesus

Christ would make sense to them. It would be "the white man's way." It would never be the Motilone way. What if some committed their lives to Jesus? Would they end up like the Orinoco Indians, bringing divisions among the Motilones, destroying their social structures?

But they *needed* Jesus. How could I introduce them to Him for what He really was, independent of my own personality and culture?

Jesus would have to do it for me. There was no other way. Nothing I could say would have the right message, the right force. But Jesus could speak through me, and He could show me the right time to speak.

I bowed my head. The sun was hot on the back of my neck. "Oh, Jesus, these people need You. Show Yourself to them. Take me out of the way, and speak to them in their own language, so that they see You for who You are.

"Oh, Jesus, become a Motilone."

17

Jesus, the Motilone

We had been on the trail three days, and were nearing Norecayra. It was late afternoon. Bobby and two other Motilones were ahead of me, their dark brown bodies hidden from view by the thick vines and bushes of the jungle. It was a beautiful time of day. The approaching darkness made the greens of the jungle soft and velvet-like.

We were walking fast. In a few miles we would reach the communal home. I began to hear loud shouts ahead of us, excruciating yells that sounded as though they came from many different mouths. I had never heard anything quite as agonizing. My steps quickened, and I began to mentally sort out the medicine in my pack.

The cries seemed more desperate as we approached. I had never heard Motilones cry out like that. They never even whimpered under the greatest pain. But Bobby and the other Motilones kept walking straight ahead on the trails, as though nothing were wrong.

"Stop!" I said. Bobby and the others turned around.

"What's that shouting?" I asked. "Shouldn't we see if there's anything we can do?"

Bobby looked down at the trail. One of the other men, who was a witch doctor, shook his head. "There's nothing we can do."

"But what's going on there?"

None of the three said anything. They stared at me with dark, quiet eyes.

As the cries continued to echo through the jungle, I got a little agitated. "Well, look," I said, "maybe you don't care about whoever that is, but I do. I want to see if we can help."

They still didn't answer me. *They're sad,* I thought. *There's something over there that is too sad for them to bear.*

"Well," I said, "you don't have to come with me. But I want to see."

They stood motionless until I turned and walked off the trail into the jungle, toward the sounds. After I had gone a few yards I heard noises behind me. They were following.

The shouting men were closer than I had thought. And there were only two of them. One I knew well. He was a leader in his communal home, and a fierce warrior. He had killed oil company employees just to get their safety helmets to use in cooking. He wore a necklace of buttons from his victims' clothes, and another necklace of jaguar teeth from a jaguar he had killed with his bow and arrow. Now, standing in front of a hole that he had dug—a hole that was a good six feet deep—he was shouting in a desperate, searching voice, "God, God, come out of the hole."

The other man was in the top of a high tree. He was stuffing leaves into his mouth and trying to chew them, while shouting, "God, God, come from the horizon!"

It was the strangest sight I had ever seen. It could have been laughable, but something kept me from seeing any humor in it.

My three companions came up alongside me, looking sad and embarrassed.

"You knew about this?" I asked Bobby.

He nodded.

"What's the matter?"

He explained that the brother of the man shouting into the hole had died in a region that was not his home. He had been bitten by a poisonous snake and had died before there was time to get him back. That meant, according to their traditions, that his language, his spirit, his life, could never go to God beyond the horizon. Now the man was trying to look for God, to get him to bring his brother's language back to life, to live in his body.

"And what makes him think he can find God by calling into a hole?"

Bobby shrugged. "It's as good a place as any to look." The hopelessness of his expression was transmitted to his words.

This was why God had let me live. I was there to tell them where they could find God. Perhaps this was an opportunity God had arranged. My body tightened at the thought of having a chance to share Christ after five years of waiting. Yet it seemed too much to expect. Inside I was praying.

The man stopped shouting into the hole, and came over to us. His hair was disheveled, his body covered with dirt. His eyes were holes into black space. "It's no point," he said. "We've been deceived."

"How long have you been here?" I asked quietly.

"Since the sun came up this morning."

"And why do you say that you've been deceived?"

He told me again the story of the false prophet that the Motilones had followed, whose false promises had led them away from God. "We no longer know God," he said quietly.

Then the other men tried to explain a Motilone legend that confirmed why this brother's death had such terrifying implications. I didn't understand it all. Motilone legends are as complicated as any theology. But I did understand something new: their great sense of lostness. I had wondered again and again what Christ had to offer them. Their way of getting along with each other was far superior to that of Americans. But there was more to life than that.

I thought of the night Jesus had entered my life. It had

been so many years before, such a small point in time. Yet it was the root out of which everything I was had grown. Through it God had brought me peace, and real purpose.

And here were the Motilones in a search for God. But how could I explain things like grace, sacrifice, the incarnation? I could tell a simple story, and they would understand. But how could I communicate real spiritual truth?

A lively discussion started. The man who had been in the trees came down and joined us. He reminded us of the legend about the prophet who would come carrying banana stalks, and that God would come out of those stalks.

I couldn't quite understand the idea behind the legend. "Why look for God to come out of a banana stalk?" I asked.

There was a puzzled silence. It made sense to them, but they couldn't explain it. Bobby walked over to a banana tree which was growing nearby. He cut off a section and tossed it toward us.

"This is the kind of banana stalk God can come from," he said. It was a cross section from the stalk. It rolled at our feet.

One of the Motilones reached down and swatted at it with his machete, accidentally splitting it in half. One half stood up, while the other half split off. Leaves that were still inside the stalk, waiting to develop and come out, started peeling off. As they lay at the base of the stalk, they looked like pages from a book.

Suddenly a word raced through my mind. "Book! Book!"

I grabbed up my pack and took out my Bible. I opened it. Flipping through the pages, I held it toward the men. I pointed to the leaves from the banana stalk, then back to the Bible.

"This is it!" I said. "I have it here! This is God's banana stalk."

One of the Motilones, the one who had been in the tree, grabbed the Bible out of my hand. He started to rip out pages and stuff them in his mouth. He thought that if he ate the pages he would have God inside him.

When nothing happened, they began to ask me questions. How could I explain the Gospel to them? How could I explain that God, in Jesus, had been like them?

Suddenly I remembered one of their legends about a man who had become an ant. He had been sitting on the trail after a hunt, and had noticed some ants trying to build a home. He'd wanted to help them make a good home, like the Motilone home, so he'd begun digging in the dirt. But because he was so big and so unknown, the ants had been afraid and had run away.

Then, quite miraculously, he had become an ant. He thought like an ant, looked like an ant, and spoke the language of an ant. He lived with the ants and they came to trust him.

He told them one day that he was not really an ant, but a Motilone, and that he had once tried to help them improve their home, but had scared them.

The ants said their equivalent of, "No kidding? That was you?" And they laughed at him, because he didn't look like the huge and fearful thing that had moved the dirt before.

But at that moment he was turned back into a Motilone, and began to move the dirt into the shape of a Motilone home. This time the ants recognized him and let him do his work, because they knew he wouldn't harm them. That was why, according to the story, the ants had hills that looked like Motilone homes.

As the story flashed into my mind, for the first time I realized its lesson: If you are big and powerful, you have to become small and weak in order to work with other weak beings. It was a perfect parallel for what God had done in Jesus.

But there were so many unknown factors in the way the Motilones reasoned. How could I be sure that I would convey the right thing?

I couldn't. Yet I felt sure God had given me this time to speak. So I took the word for "becoming like an ant," and used it for incarnation. "God is incarnated into man," I said.

They gasped. There was a tense, hushed silence. The idea that God had become a man stunned them.

"Where did He walk?" the witch doctor asked in a whisper.

Every Motilone has his own trail. It is his personal point of identity. You walk on someone's trail if you want to find him. God would have a trail, too. If you want to find God you walk on His trail.

My blood was racing, my heart pounding. "Jesus Christ is God become man," I said. "He can show you God's trail."

A look of astonishment, almost of fear, spread over their faces. The man who had been shouting into the hole looked at me.

"Show us Christ," he said in a coarse whisper.

I fumbled for an answer. "You killed Christ," I said. "You destroyed God."

His eyes got big. "I killed Christ? I did that? How did I do that? And how can God be killed?"

I wanted to tell them that Jesus' death had freed them from meaninglessness, from death and the powers of evil.

"How does evil, death, and deception find power over the Motilone people?" I asked.

"Through the ears," Bobby answered, because language is so important to the Motilones. It is the essence of life. If evil language comes through the ears, it means death.

"Do you remember," I said, "how after a hunt for wild boars the leader cuts the skin from the animal and puts it over his head, to cover his ears and keep the evil spirits of the jungle out?"

They nodded, listening closely.

"Jesus Christ was murdered," I said. "But just as you pull the skin over the chieftain's head to hide his ears, so Jesus—when he died—pulled His blood over your deception and hides it from the sight of God."

I stood looking at them, hoping desperately that they would understand. Then I saw on their faces that they did.

I told them that Jesus was buried. A wave of grief swept over them. The man who was searching for his brother's language began to weep. It was the first time I had ever seen a Motilone cry. But the thought that God was dead, that they were lost, brought tears and sobs.

I picked up my Bible, opened it, and said, "The Bible speaks that Jesus came alive after death, and is alive today."

One of the men grabbed the Bible from my hand and put it to his ear. "I can't hear a thing," he said.

I took it back. "The way the Bible speaks does not change," I said. "It is like the papers of your speech that I have. They say the same word one day to the next. The Bible says that Jesus came to life. It is God's banana stalk."

I showed him the page, and told him that the little black markings had meaning.

"No one has ever come back from the dead in all Motilone history," he said.

"I know," I replied. "But Jesus did. It is proof that He is really God's Son."

They asked many more questions. Some I didn't fully understand. But I was sure that God had spoken through me. That night I prayed, "God, give validity to Your Word. Make it touch these lives." I claimed God's promise that His Word would not return to Him without any response.

Yet there didn't seem to be any response. I continued to walk the trails with Bobby, giving medicine to the witch doctors, and showing them how to do their work more effectively.

One evening, though, Bobby began to ask questions. We were sitting around a fire. The light flickered over him. His face was serious.

"How can I walk on Jesus' trail?" he asked. "No Motilone has ever done it. It's a new thing. There is no other Motilone to tell how to do it."

I remembered the problems I had had as a boy, how it sometimes appeared impossible to keep on believing in Jesus when my family and friends were so opposed to my commitment. That was what Bobby was going through.

"Bobby," I said, "do you remember my first Festival of the Arrows, the first time I had seen all the Motilones gathered to sing their song?" The festival was the most important ceremony in the Motilone culture.

He nodded. The fire flared up momentarily and I could see his eyes, staring intently at me.

"Do you remember that I was afraid to climb in the high hammocks to sing, for fear that the rope would break? And I told you that I would sing only if I could have one foot in the hammock and one foot on the ground?"

"Yes, Bruchko."

"And what did you say to me?"

He laughed. "I told you you had to have both feet in the hammock. 'You have to be suspended,' I said."

"Yes," I said. "You have to be suspended. That is how it is when you follow Jesus, Bobby. No man can tell you how to walk His trail. Only Jesus can. But to find out you have to tie your hammock strings into Him, and be suspended in God."

Bobby said nothing. The fire danced in his eyes. Then he stood up and walked off into the darkness.

The next day he came to me. "Bruchko," he said, "I want to tie my hammock strings into Jesus Christ. But how can I? I can't see Him or touch Him."

"You have talked to spirits, haven't you?"

"Oh," he said. "I see now."

The next day he had a big grin on his face. "Bruchko, I've tied my hammock strings into Jesus. Now I speak a new language."

I didn't understand what he meant. "Have you learned some of the Spanish I speak?"

He laughed, a clean, sweet laugh. "No, Bruchko, I *speak* a new language."

Then I understood. To a Motilone, language is life. If Bobby had a new life, he had a new way of speaking. His speech would be Christ-oriented.

We put our hands on each other's shoulders. My mind swept back to the first time I had met Jesus, and the life I had felt flow into me. Now my brother Bobby was experiencing Jesus himself, in the same way. He had begun to walk with Jesus.

"Jesus Christ has risen from the dead!" Bobby shouted, so that the sound filtered far off into the jungle. "He has walked our trails.! I have met Him!"

From that day our friendship was enhanced by our love for Jesus. We talked constantly about Him, and Bobby asked me many questions. But he never asked the color of Jesus' hair, or whether He had blue eyes. To Bobby, the answers were obvious: Jesus had dark skin, and His eyes were black. He wore a G-string, and hunted with bows and arrows.

Jesus was a Motilone.

18

The Night of the Tiger

I was lying in my hammock after the morning hunt. The women were cooking, and the acrid smoke of the fires, mixed with the smell of roasting monkey, made me drowsy. Soon it would be time to eat. I was hungry.

I heard a commotion in the other end of the home, and lifted myself up on my elbow to see what was happening. A little knot of men and women had gathered around Abacuriana, a young, slender, man. I caught a few of his words.

"Tiger . . . I couldn't move . . . ." He was talking excitedly.

Two men in hammocks near me got up and started toward the cluster of people. "Hey, Chanti." I called to one of them. "What's going on?"

He came over to my hammock. He seemed nervous. "Didn't you hear?" he asked hoarsely. "The tiger spoke."

"What tiger?" I said, confused. "Spoke what? What are you talking about?"

"The tiger spoke! He spoke!"

I shook my head. "Chanti, tigers don't speak. And if they did, who would care what they said?"

"Oh," he said, "when the tiger speaks we are in big trouble. Big, big trouble."

By this time, his eyes were rolling. "Okay, thanks," I said, and let him go.

The whole house was in an uproar. All work stopped. Those who couldn't get close to Abacuriana stood on the perimeter of the crowd and talked, or walked swiftly to the door and stared outside.

I got out of my hammock. The chief was standing at one of the doors. I drew him aside.

"I want to talk to you," I said. "What does it mean that the tiger spoke?"

"It means we're in for big trouble," he said.

"But what kind of trouble? What could a tiger say that would be dangerous?"

"I'm going into the jungle to talk to the tiger. He'll tell me."

"But chief," I said, "tigers don't talk. This is nonsense."

He gave me a quick, hard glance. "Look," he said, "you don't know anything about the jungle. You don't know how to hunt, you don't know what to eat. You can't keep up on the trail. What makes you think you know anything about tigers?"

There wasn't much I could say. I looked at him in nervous astonishment, while he stared coldly into the jungle. Then, with monumental effort, he squared his shoulders and walked out of the house. I watched him cross the clearing and disappear, alone, into the trees. I turned. Everyone in the home was looking at the area where he had disappeared.

He was gone until late afternoon. Everyone waited for him to return. No one worked. A few men tried to carve arrows, but they would stop often and stare into space. There was very little talking. People walked restlessly around the house, and their restlessness was transferred to me. I couldn't sit still. What was going on? I had never seen anything like this. The house seemed to be pressed down by a huge, invisible hand.

When the chief came back, people immediately huddled around him. He waited to speak until everyone had gathered. His face was tired and drawn. He seemed to have aged ten years.

"The tiger says that the spirits will come out of the rocks tonight. They will attack this home. Lives will be snuffed out. Languages will cease. There will be death."

In profound silence, the chief walked off and got in his hammock. People wandered off by themselves.

What on earth is going on? I wondered. *Where did all this fear come from? What does it mean, that the tiger speaks and spirits come out of the rocks?*

It was obvious that something really terrifying was happening. These people were not normally superstitious, and I had never never seen them really frightened before. They routinely faced poisonous snakes and dangerous animals, and never showed a trace of fear. If they were afraid now, there must be something worth being afraid of. But what was it? How could they fight it?

I found Bobby outside the home, staring off into the distance. He glanced over at me when I came up.

"Bruchko, can Jesus be taken out of my mouth?" he asked, a tense edge of fear in his voice.

"Bobby, what is this all about? What does it mean that the tiger speaks? What does it mean that the spirits will come out of the rocks?"

"The spirits come out of the rocks," he said. "They try to kill. Sometimes only one dies. Sometimes many die. In Ocbabuda two months ago seven died."

"How do they die?" I asked. "What kills them?"

"The spirits kill them, Bruchko," he said. "They die in their hammocks because the evil spirits tear their language away from them."

"Bobby, does someone always die?"

"Always," he said.

The air seemed thick. What did this mean? Why did I feel under so much pressure?

"Can Jesus be taken out of my mouth?" Bobby asked again, looking out into the jungle.

I didn't know how to answer him. I had never before dealt with demon powers. I felt frightened, too.

"Can the devil kill me now that I walk in Jesus' path?" he continued. "Bruchko, what am I to do?"

"I don't know, Bobby. You'll have to talk to Jesus yourself. He is the only one who has the answer to your questions. He will speak to you in your heart."

He hesitated, then walked off into the jungle. I immediately felt regret. Why hadn't I given him some advice? What kind of spiritual father was I?

But I didn't have any advice to give.

I went for a long walk into the jungle. I was not only frightened but confused. "Tigers can't talk," I told God. "What is happening here?"

When I got back to the home it was nearly dark. As soon as I entered the clearing I heard strange, high wailings and incantations. The house was swaying back and forth, as if possessed by the devil himself. The incantations were jumbled. They went up and down, gathering force, then dropping. The air seemed electric. I was almost afraid to enter.

Inside the fires cast an eerie red glow. I saw that the house indeed was swaying. All the men, high up in their hammocks, were swinging and chanting to ward off the devil. The women were on the floor, clapping large rocks together. Their eyes—like the eyes of the men—were tightly closed.

Where was Bobby? Was he in this place? Suddenly I was afraid for him. He was the only Motilone who had begun to walk Jesus' trail. Had he given in to this fear and superstition?

Then I saw his hammock. He was in it, swinging. I almost turned back and into the jungle. But something restrained me. He was my brother.

I grasped one of the poles that supported the house and began to shinny up toward Bobby's hammock which was almost twenty feet above the floor. The bamboo bent under my weight and I wondered if it would hold me. But Bobby's welfare was the most important thing in the world to me just then. Hand over hand, I pulled myself up. When I got high enough, I looked into Bobby's hammock. His eyes were open. He had a big smile on his face. The song he was singing was different:

"Jesus is in my mouth;
I have a new speech.
Jesus is in my mouth;
no one can take Him from me.
I speak Jesus' words.
I walk in Jesus' steps.
I am a Jesus' boy;
He has filled my stomach, and I am no longer hungry."

As I clung to the palm tree pole, Bobby looked straight at me. He was safe. He knew Jesus. He was doing the thing I should have had the vision to suggest. He was keeping the evil spirits away by singing a song of Jesus.

I joined him in the song. All that night we sang. When dawn came, no one had died. It was the first time in anyone's memory that the spirits had walked and no one had died.

No one commented on Bobby's song, yet I could sense that the other Motilones had a new interest in him and in his relationship to Jesus. It wasn't particularly outward; that wasn't the Motilone way. But the evidence was clear.

And Bobby began to change. In the months that followed his commitment to Jesus, he became less proud. When he visited other homes, he accepted food immediately instead of forcing himself to go without it to demonstrate his strength. That stubbornness had not made him very popular among the other men, though they respected him for it. Now they noticed his new attitude and wondered what caused it.

I was eager for Bobby to tell them. He could do it more effectively than I, I was sure. I tried to encourage him to share his experiences, and was upset when he didn't. Was it because he didn't care enough about the other Motilones? I couldn't be sure.

But I was trying to squeeze him into "the mold," and didn't realize it. News has no real significance to the Motilones until it's given in a formal ceremony. In my excitement over Bobby's spiritual experience, I wanted him to do things the way they would have been done in North America. I wanted him to call a meeting and tell about

Jesus, or corner his friends and explain what Jesus now meant to him. But thank God he waited until he could do it the Motilone way.

Word spread that there was to be another Festival of the Arrows. There was excitement in the home. The Festival was the only time all the Motilones gathered together.

Pacts would be formed. Arrows would be exchanged, and the men forming the pact would have a singing contest. They would climb into their hammocks and sing as long as they could, relating legends, stories, and news of recent events. Often their songs would last twelve hours, without interruption for food, water, or rest.

People streamed into the home. There was lots of noise and food. Old friends greeted each other, and swapped stories. People were looking at Bobby in a new light. Word had spread about the night the spirits had walked and no one had died. He was looked on with respect, and some curiosity. He had married, and was accepted as a man.

An older chief named Adjibacbayra took a special interest in Bobby. His reserved air made him appear dignified. However, he had a lot of curiosity, and on the first day of the Festival, challenged Bobby to a song. Bobby was pleased, and immediately accepted.

They both climbed into a single hammock twenty feet off the ground, and began to swing back and forth. Bobby sang first, and Adjibacbayra imitated him, following line for line. Other men also had challenged each other to songs, and were singing.

Bobby's song was about the way the Motilones had been deceived and had lost God's trail. He told how they had once known God, but had been greedy and had followed a false prophet. Then he began to sing about Jesus. As he did so, the other men who were singing stopped. Everyone became quiet in order to listen.

"Jesus Christ was incarnated into man," Bobby sang. "He has walked our trails. He is God yet we can know Him."

The home was deathly still, except for Bobby's wailing song and Adjibacbayra's repetition. People were straining their ears to hear.

Inside me, however, a spiritual battle was raging. I found myself hating the song. It seemed so heathen. The music, chanted in a strange minor key, sounded like witch music. It seemed to degrade the Gospel. Yet when I looked at the people around me, and up at the chief swinging in his hammock, I could see that they were listening as though their lives depended on it. Bobby was giving them spiritual truth through the song.

Still I wanted to do it *my* way . . . until I heard Bobby sing about Jesus giving him a new language.

"Can't you see the reality that he is giving to them?" God seemed to ask me.

"But Lord," I replied, "why am I so repulsed by it?"

Then I saw that it was because I was sinful. I could love the Motilone way of life, but when it came to spiritual matters I thought I had the only way. But my way wasn't necessarily God's way. God was saying, "I too love the Motilone way of life. I made it. And I'm going to tell them about my Son in *my* way."

I relaxed, able at last to find real joy in Bobby's song. It continued for eight hours, ten hours. Attention didn't slacken. It got dark inside the house. Fires were built. Finally, after fourteen hours, they quit singing and climbed wearily down from their hammock.

Adjibacbayra looked at Bobby. "You've communicated a true news item," he said. "I too want to suspend myself in Jesus. I want to pull His blood over my deception."

That night a spiritual revolution swept over the people. No one rejected the news about Jesus. Everyone wanted Him to take them over the horizon. There was tremendous jubilation. Sometimes it was quiet and people would talk to each other in little groups. At other times, the joy would break into spontaneous singing. It went late into the night.

God had spoken. He had spoken in the Motilone language, and through the Motilone culture. He had not even had to use me.

19

Everyday Miracles

It seemed a miracle that the Motilones had accepted Jesus at the Festival of the Arrows. A song of praise filled my heart for days.

Then I heard news from other Festivals of the Arrows. The words Bobby had sung had been repeated there and had been joyfully accepted. It was almost more than I could believe.

As people began responding to the Word and obeying God, other things happened that I also called "miracles"— things that were clearly supernatural. But the Motilone idea of a miracle wasn't necessarily mine. Some things that astounded me they took in stride.

Medicine, for instance. After the Motilones began to walk with Jesus, there was a tremendous expansion in that field. But whenever shots, pills or ointments were administered, they were accompanied by a chant that called on Jesus to heal. For the Motilones, the healing that the medicine accomplished was a miracle from Jesus.

It was something He did for them. Their prayers were a part of the healing process.

Sometimes that brought surprising results. One day I arrived at a home to find a man who, the week before, had been bitten by a poisonous snake. He had almost recovered.

"I thought you were out of snake anti-venom," I said. "Where did you get some?"

"We didn't have any," the witch doctor replied.

"What, in heaven's name, did you do to make him recover?"

"Well, all we had was some antibiotic. So we gave him that and prayed that God would heal him. As you can see, He did."

I was astonished. The antibiotic was absolutely no good for snake poisoning. God had healed the man, not the medicine.

But wasn't that what the Motilones said about all healings? What difference did God's method make? Whether a person used the proper medicine or not, it was still His healing.

But I was glad that God chose to work in visibly powerful ways among the Motilones, if only to show me that He really was changing their hearts. Otherwise it would have been impossible for me to believe the almost total acceptance of the Gospel on the part of the Motilones. Sometimes I would think, *Is this really true conversion, or is it just one more legend for the Motilones to draw on?* Then God would let me see the powerful changes in their lives so I could not doubt that He was working in and through them.

One day I returned from a trip to find that Atabacdora had been brought in with a fractured back. He had fallen from a tree during a monkey hunt. We had no facilities for helping him there, so we carried him over trails for three days, then floated down-stream with him to the hospital in Tibu. They X-rayed him there, and the doctor told me that he had a broken neck. He would have to lie perfectly still for months. Because I was the only person who spoke both Spanish and Motilone, I was to relay this news to him.

Atabacdora was lying on his back in bed. They had put

supports under him so that his back curved up in the middle. He was uncomfortable. The nurses, he complained, wouldn't let him move.

"The doctor just told me that you'll have to lie still for three months," I told him, "If you don't, you will never get well."

"No Bruchko," he said. "I can't do that. I can't lie here that long."

"Atabacdora, you have to. If you don't you won't get well."

I made him promise to obey the doctor's orders, but he wasn't happy about it. And I wasn't sure how long his promise would last. Bobby and I discussed it, but neither of us thought of a solution. He might lie quietly for a week, if he really tried. But three months? Impossible!

"Look, Bobby," I said, "sometimes the men who knew Jesus when He walked the trails would anoint a sick person with oil and pray that he'd be healed. I think maybe we should do that with Atabacdora."

"And does it work, Bruchko?" Bobby asked. "Does God heal in this way?"

"I don't know, Bobby. I've never tried it."

I didn't have much faith that it would really help, but I knew Atabacdora would never be able to lie still for three months, and I couldn't stand the thought of seeing him crippled for life.

We got some oil, and went into his hospital room. He was in pain. The sedatives weren't having enough effect, but he still smiled at us. "We want to pray for you," I said.

Bobby dipped his finger in the oil, then I did the same. We stood there for a moment. Bobby was waiting for me to go ahead.

"I don't know where to put the oil," I said. "Somewhere on his head, but I don't know where."

"Let's put it on his forehead," Bobby said.

We did that, then put our hands on his head. Bobby prayed.

"God," he said, "Atabacdora has a backache. He needs to be well again so that he can run the trails and fish and hunt with his brother Motilones. You can make his backache go away. We want You to do that, and we ask You to do it in the name of Jesus."

We said a few more words to Atabacdora and left.

I had some business in Cucuta, so I put Atabacdora in Bobby's hands. The business took three days. I spent most of them worrying about Atabacdora. When I got back, I immediately went to Bobby. He was annoyed.

"Atabacdora won't even try to stay still, Bruchko," he said. "He says he's uncomfortable lying on his back, and he won't stay flat."

We went to the hospital to see him. His bed was empty. I was alarmed. Had he hurt himself by moving around, and been taken to the operating room for surgery?

Then Atabacdora walked into the room. When he saw us he got a guilty look on his face, like a child who's been caught stealing cookies. Quickly, without a word, he got into bed and made a show of lying correctly, with his back curved up in the middle. He had no sooner assumed that pose than a red-faced nurse came in behind him, huffing. Pointing at him and sputtering, she reprimanded me loudly for letting him get out of bed. Atabacdora lay quite still, with a beatific look on his face. When the nurse finally left, threatening all kinds of evil, he grinned.

It was my turn to scold. "Atabacdora, don't you care about getting well? If you don't lie still you may never be able to hunt again."

He pouted. "Bruchko, I just couldn't stay in the bed any longer. It's uncomfortable. I did what you said for three days, but that was enough."

"Bruchko," Bobby said, "if he doesn't have his backache any more, why should he stay in bed?"

I hadn't thought of that. I found the doctor, and asked him if he would take another X-ray of Atabacdora. He didn't want to, but I wheedled him into it. "All right," he said. "If it'll make you happy I'll do it."

The next day he came up to me with a puzzled look. "Is that the same Indian you brought in originally?"

"Of course," I said. "Do you think we play checkers with your patients?"

"Well, if it is the same man, his back has mended. It's quite amazing. There's no sign of even a hairline fracture in his back now. It's some kind of a miracle."

"Boy," he said. "I want to find out what his exact treatment was. I've never known our treatment to be so effective."

I laughed. "You don't think that there was something more than medicine working here?"

"Like what?" he asked.

"Like God."

He went off shaking his head.

I was tremendously elated. I found Bobby and told him what had happened. "Bobby, do you realize that it's a miracle?"

Bobby wasn't excited. To him it was just a backache that God had healed. Lots of people got backaches, lay in their hammock for a day, then got up and went about their business. This one was a little worse than usual.

"But, Bobby," I said, "The X-ray showed that his neck was *broken*."

"What's an X-ray?"

"Well, I can't explain that, Bobby. But the point is that God healed him."

"But, Bruchko, why is that a surprise? We have seen too many people healed to be surprised at any more."

In 1967, about a year after the first Motilones had become Christians, Arabadoyca and a small group of other men came to talk to me. They had decided that they wanted to tell the Yuko Indians about Jesus. I had had the same desire earlier, and had made a trip back to the Yuko village where I had spent nearly a year.

I hadn't been there more than an hour before I saw that something had changed. I soon discovered what it was. One of the women whom I had tried to tell about Jesus when I was there the first time had had a vision. As a result, most of the village had accepted Jesus. They had given up chicha, the drink they had gotten drunk on so often, and there was a noticeably different quality of life in the village. Instead of telling the Yukos about Jesus, as I'd set out to do, they told me about Him.

However, I was surprised to learn that the Motilones wanted to talk to the Yukos about Jesus. The two tribes had been bitter enemies for years. The Yukos had a game they liked to play. They would braid the long, five-inch jungle thorns and lay them on the Motilone trails. Then they would hide in the brush and wait. When a Motilone ran along the trail, he would step on the thorns. The Yukos would laugh at his agony and run away.

Now Motilones wanted to tell Yukos about Jesus. At that time they didn't understand that there were languages other than the Motilone language. They thought that the Yukos spoke just like they did. But the languages are totally different. I couldn't see how they would manage to communicate anything about Jesus.

But I wasn't going to try to restrain them. I suggested that they go to the lowland tribes, who hadn't heard about Jesus. A few days later, they left. I prayed that it wouldn't be a shattering experience for them, that God would comfort them in any disappointment at being unable to communicate.

They were gone for several weeks. When they got back I went to see Arabadoyca, curious about what had happened.

"How did it go?" I asked.

He was making arrows, and he looked up at me with his familiar crooked grin. "Wonderful," he said. "They had not known about Jesus before."

"And did they understand?"

"Oh, yes, we told them a great many things about Jesus."

"You spoke to them?"

"Of course." Arabadoyca was a little concerned about my surprise. "How would you have told them?"

"Oh . . . in the same way. But how do you know they understood?"

Again he looked perplexed. "Why, they told us that they did. They were very excited to hear the news, Bruchko."

"You mean you opened your mouth and spoke to the Yukos and they understood you, and they talked to you and you understood them?"

"Yes, of course."

The Yuko language is not a dialect of the Motilone language. It is a totally different language. You could never understand the one from knowing the other. Yet I am sure that Arabadoyca and the others were not lying. Lying is almost unknown among the Motilones. And they had no reason to lie. There is also the fact that there now are Christians in the Yuko lowland where there were none before.

I can only conclude that God's Holy Spirit made the Motilones speak and understand Yuko. It was a miracle to me. But to the Motilones, everything that God does is a miracle.

I have learned, with the Motilones, to expect God to provide what we need, regardless of circumstances. On one occasion, when we were fighting a measles epidemic, I ran out of drugs. Measles is one of the deadliest diseases for the Indians, and without antibiotics I was helpless. There already were ten cases of measles, and it was spreading fast.

But I felt sure that God would provide the drugs somehow. I never doubted that, even though I had no funds in the bank, no credit.

I went into Tibu, sure that there would be some money. I opened all my mail. There wasn't a cent.

I still felt sure that God had an answer to the problem. He had before in similar circumstances, and His spirit was comforting me about this particular case.

I went into Cucuta, opened my post office box there, and found a check for five hundred dollars.

It didn't shock me. I merely said, "Thank goodness, it's come." I cashed it, then bought the medicine I needed. The bill came to five hundred and sixty five dollars.

"I have five hundred dollars here, and if you wait I'll pay the rest," I told the clerk. He agreed. It was a big sale, and he didn't want to pass it up.

The day before I left Cucuta I checked the post office box again. There was a check for one hundred dollars. I paid the drug supply house their money, and had some left over to buy a good meal and some things I would need in the jungle. Then I went back to Tibu, and from there into the jungle. The drugs were enough to stop the epidemic and control its complications.

The greatest miracle I have seen, though, has been the changed life of the Motilones. They have found their purpose in Jesus Christ. As a result, they have broken down the individuality that prevented them from helping each other. There is real caring for others; real self-sacrifice. That has made their economic development possible as well as their spiritual development. Without it, their programs always bogged down. With it, their problems are being solved.

I have spoken before the United Nations. I have spoken to the Organization of American States. I have been a personal friend of the last four presidents of Colombia. My experience with the Motilone Indians has taught me how to deal with other cultures; how to promote positive change without tearing social structures apart at the seams. I try to share these things. But the most important thing that I can say to those who want to help primitive people is this: They will not be helped very much unless they find purpose in life through Jesus Christ. Without Him, whatever development takes place always will be twisted or corrupted. It will embitter those who try to hold it together, and those who don't care about it will be ruined by apathy and alienation.

But with Jesus, there can be real change. Not just spiritual change. Not just change by and by. Real change, now, with visible power. He is the source of all change. He is the God of everyday miracles.

20

Like David and Jonathan

George Camibocbayra met me outside the home, and took me aside. "You had better go and see Bobby right away," he said. "His daughter is very sick, and they've taken her to the hospital at Tibu."

I ducked into the home and found Bobby sitting on a mat, looking down at his feet. His face was sad. I put a hand on his shoulder. He looked up, then back down at his feet.

"I heard that your daughter is sick," I said.

He nodded. "We took her to Tibu three days ago."

"Why did you come back here?"

"I have my wife to care for. She is pregnant, you know. And I have duties to carry out, bringing in supplies and taking out things to sell. And what good could I be in Tibu?"

"And yet," I said, smiling slightly, "it doesn't look as though you're much good here, either."

He looked up at me again. His face seemed tired and aged. "No, that's true," he said. "I can't stop thinking about her."

He stood up beside me. I glanced over at Atacadara, his wife. She was standing, watching Bobby with great concern. Her stomach was swelled out in pregnancy, but she still had the slender face and dark eyes of a beautiful woman. She loved Bobby. Even with her daughter sick and taken away from her, she was most concerned about Bobby.

I looked back at Bobby. "Let's pray together about your daughter," I said. "Then I'll go down to Tibu to see if I can be of any help. You should stay here to care for Atacadara."

Four days later I was standing over the little girl's bed. Her body seemed deflated. Her skin hung on her bones, and her eyes had a thin film over them.

The doctor was standing beside me. "What disease does she have?" I asked.

He was a young fellow just out of medical school. "We don't know," he said. "It may be a combination of several things. I don't know if we're going to be able to do much for her."

A cold chill ran down to my fingertips. "You mean she's going to die?"

"Who knows?" he said. "If we can't find out what's the matter with her, she probably will."

I walked out of the hospital thinking of how Bobby used to lift her up to my hammock. I would set her on my stomach and sing songs to her, while she smiled and made googling noises.

I remembered when Bobby had married Atacadara. It was soon after he had accepted Christ. Atacadara had been the prettiest and most intelligent girl in the home. Bobby had let her know through a friend that he liked her. They had blushed every time they had seen each other. Atacadara was infatuated with Bobby. He was a handsome, strong young warrior, the prize catch, you might say, of the tribe.

One day she had moved her hammock next to Bobby's, and they had been married. Her father had been angry. He wasn't at all interested in a son-in-law. He wanted his daughter to stay in the family. But she had refused.

I laughed when I thought about how I had felt then. I had been afraid that Bobby's marriage would interrupt our friendship, that we'd never be really close again. But it had worked just the opposite. Atacadara and I had become brother and sister, and when their first daughter was born I was her second father according to Motilone custom. We had become a family.

Bobby was a devoted father and husband. It wasn't common for Motilone men to share much with their wives, but Bobby and Atacadara were close from the beginning of their marriage. It was Bobby's talking that, even before the Festival of the Arrows, brought her to know Christ. They weren't just man and wife, they were friends. Often they would lie in the same hammock and talk for hours. You would hear their low voices murmuring across the communal home until late in the night.

Now their little girl was on the edge of death. But God had to heal her. She meant too much to Bobby and Atacadara.

The next day when the doctor told me that she had died in the night, it was like a slap in the face.

I had to tell Bobby. When he heard, his face went pale. Without saying a word, he walked into the jungle, and didn't come back until that night. Even then, he didn't speak or show any sign of affection for Atacadara or for me. Two days later, Atacadara gave birth to another girl, but Bobby mustered only a weak recognition. Every day he took long walks in the jungle. When he returned he wouldn't mention where he had been. If I spoke to him, he usually didn't respond.

It was his first real trial as a Christian and it was a hard one. He continued to show no sign of love for Atacadara or for his new child. We prayed for him, but for two long weeks there was only heavy remorse.

Then he began to notice his new daughter. I took her over to him and placed her in his arms. He held and rocked her. Within a week he was carrying her everywhere, and he and Atacadara were closer than ever. Everyone noticed their oneness. Bobby's father-in-law, who had stayed quite bitter about the marriage, began to eat meals with them. He could see that he had been wrong. Later he became a Christian mainly because of the marriage relationship his daughter had found.

Bobby's family grew, too. Within another year he had

his first son, and that made him very happy. But he wasn't selfish with his family. I had thought he might spend all his time working for them instead of for the other Motilones. The opposite seemed to happen: his love for his family seemed to overflow to everyone else, so that he was more interested than ever in helping others.

On one of our trips to the higher Motilone territory we met a boy of about eight named Odo. The boy's entire family had died in an epidemic, so he had no one, and was developing into a juvenile delinquent. He went from communal home to communal home, always finding something to eat, but never being really accepted.

He wasn't a pleasant boy. He took it for granted that he should be fed and taken care of, and he wasn't thankful when someone did. He also upset things and frequently got into trouble.

Bobby and I had both noticed him, but since we were just passing through, I didn't think much about him. Bobby, however, did. He told me one day that he would be bringing Odo along when we left.

"What for, Bobby? He'll just get in our way."

"He needs somebody," Bobby said. "Maybe if he comes with us he can help us, and we'll be able to help him."

When we suggested that Odo come with us, he got suspicious. "Why do you want me to come?"

Bobby ignored his suspicion. "We need some extra help. There's a lot of work to be done, and it's too much for the two of us. You're smart, anyone can see that, so we figure you'll catch on quickly."

Odo looked back and forth at us, trying to see what we wanted from him. Finally he nodded his head. "All right," he said.

It wasn't easy to put up with him at first. Bobby's patience amazed me. He never got angry or visibly upset. Within a few weeks, I began to notice a change in Odo's attitude. He stayed near Bobby constantly. Instead of being in our way he actually began to be a help. When we returned to our communal home, Odo came with us and became part of Bobby's family. Whereas before he had been filthy, he began to wash, even though Bobby had never said a word to him about it. Within a few months he was being noticed by people, not for his bad behavior, but for the fact that he was a precocious young man. In imitating Bobby, he became concerned for others.

This period was one of the most relaxed and enjoyable I had ever had. Bobby and I were constantly together. There were no secrets between us. I could see that he was becoming the outstanding young leader of the Motilones. I never had to tell him what to do. In fact, when he came to me for advice, I would tell him that he had to decide for himself. Other young men who had come to know Christ and who had a concern for others began to work with us. A system of leadership developed. It was great to see the work progress. Crops were developed, sick people cured, and more and more Motilones found their real identity in Christ.

Best of all was the time that I spent with Bobby. The Bible says of David that his love for Jonathan was "more than the love he had for any woman." I had never understood that. But there is a perfect brotherly love, and as this love for Bobby grew, I stopped worrying about where it would lead. I just wanted to spend time with him, and with his family, and enjoy the things that God had given us together.

Perhaps our best times came after the evening meal, when we would sit around the fire or lie in our hammocks, Bobby and Atacadara close together, Odo and me nearby, with Bobby's children passed from one person to the other, chortling and giggling. We would sing the Motilone songs, and talk about the things that had happened during the day. If we had a good meal we would rub our stomachs, and I might walk over to Bobby and pat his stomach and laugh. There were jokes, and legends of the Motilone past, and always stories about Jesus and the things He had done when He had walked the Motilone trails as a man. Sometimes I would take out my Bible and would tell them about a passage. Eventually the fires would die down, the air would grow quiet and the nightly rain would begin to fall. One by one we would drift off to sleep.

One day Bobby asked me whether we could make the Bible so that the Motilone people could understand it for themselves. They wanted to know more about Jesus. By then I was spending quite a bit of time just telling them about

Him and answering their questions. I knew that I couldn't translate the Bible into their idioms by myself, because I still didn't have a complete understanding of the language and of the Motilone legends. But with Bobby's help it was possible, because there were no barriers to our communication.

So we began to translate the book of Mark. It is one thing to learn to speak a new language, quite another to put a complete book like a Gospel into that language. In trips out of the jungle I got volumes on linguistics and translating and met a young man from Corscas who became interested in using a computer to help in the translation. Since my long-term interest had been linguistics, it was exciting to be involved with it.

The most exciting part of the work, however, was the actual translation that I did with Bobby. Once a written Motilone language was established, there still was the problem of making Biblical phrases understandable. That is where Bobby helped.

How do you tell a primitive tribe about things like grace when they have no such word in their vocabulary? Sometimes I would try to adapt a Christian idea to the Motilone culture. I already had had success with the word *faith* which I had related to suspending your hammock from Christ, and the word *incarnation* which I had related to the legend about the Motilone who became an ant. If my new effort was a good one, Bobby would say so. Other times he would say, "No, that's not right, Bruchko. Jesus is not like that," and I would have to try again.

He also filled me in on some of the aspects of the culture that I hadn't fully understood. The Motilone, for instance, always use names that have a meaning. There are no names like Kent or Kim that are names and nothing more. So Bible characters had to be given names that made sense. Abraham became the "Man Who Knows God," John the Baptist became the "Announcer" and "Jungle Dweller," and Jesus "The only Son of God with us." Every time a name had to be given, we spent long hours around the fire discussing the person and what kind of a name would be best for him. Often other Motilones would join us and would help with the decision.

Some parables didn't seem to fit the Motilone culture, either. Take, for example, the parable of the man who built his house on rock so that it would be firm. When Bobby first heard it, he suggested that it be deleted.

"That's not right, Bruchko. A house that is solid must be built on sand. Otherwise the poles won't go deep enough and the house will fall apart."

So we adjusted the parable. After all, Jesus had chosen it to clarify a truth for his listeners. Wouldn't he want the Motilones to understand also?

We were both proud when the translation was finished. However our work was just beginning: I was the only one who could read it. Bobby began to teach some of the children. We held class each afternoon outside the home, a little way into the jungle where it was cool.

But we began to hear grumbling from the older men. About a month after we had started teaching, Bobby told me we would have to stop.

I was shocked. "What for? We have just begun," I said.

"It's the older men, the leaders. They feel that it's not right to teach the children things that their elders don't know."

For an instant I was angry.

"We should stop teaching the Gospel just because of a bunch of jealous old men?" I snapped.

Bobby didn't answer. He just looked sad.

I could have shot myself for saying that. It wasn't my Gospel. It was the Motilone's Gospel. No good news should tear their social system into shreds.

We stopped teaching the children, and asked the older men to learn instead. There was great competition among them. They didn't learn as quickly as the children, but they tried.

After a month or so they felt comfortable enough to have their children learning, too. Instead of living in totally different worlds, as is so often the case between generations elsewhere, the older men and women shared their new knowledge with their children. It added to the unity of the tribe instead of destroying it.

Before long, a number of Motilones could both read and write. They rattled off the Gospel of Mark like a machine gun, the staccato syllables of the Motilone language coming out of their mouths as fast as they could speak. But there was no comprehension.

So an elderly chief suggested a rule. It was adopted, and now is used wherever classes are taught. Every time someone reads a verse, someone else asks a question about it.

For instance, a Motilone might read, "For God so loved the world that He gave his only begotten Son, that whosoever believes in Him shall not perish . . . ."

Another Motilone might ask, "Who loved the world?"

If the first man can't answer, he reads the verse again, trying to understand it. When he understands it, he begins to ask himself, "How does this affect me?"

So the work progressed. But I was getting restless again. How long would God keep me there?

21
Gloria

During my first five or six years with the Motilones, I had almost no contact with the outside world. However, while working on the translation of Mark with Bobby, I bought a transistor radio and brought it back to the communal home. For several nights I lay awake listening to the announcer talk about things that seemed almost unreal. I could remember what that other world was like, all right, but it seemed very far away.

One night I lay in my hammock, with bows and arrows for killing tomorrow's dinner nearby, and listened to the broadcast of the first men walking on the moon. Part of me wanted to pack up and go where cars and planes and streetcars ruled instead of panthers and wild boars. At the same time, I was strangely pleased with myself. It was as though I had a secret that the world did not know; a secret place that no one else had been allowed to enter.

Few people believed that I had contacted the Motilones when I first reentered the outside world. Nevertheless, some newspapers heard what I was doing, and the next time I went out to civilization several reporters found me and questioned me about my work with the Motilones. Their reports attracted quite a bit of attention. Before long the Motilones were the heroes of Colombia. Several Motilone men accompanied me on one trip out for supplies, and one of them, Axducatsyara, was named the Colombian "Man of the Year." Up until that point, all newspaper accounts of the Motilones had stressed the fact that they killed oil company employees. Gradually, however, the newspapers began to understand that, on the whole, the Motilones had simply been defending their territory against people who wanted to steal their land and destroy their way of life. Public sentiment shifted and, as so often happens, it got carried away and indiscriminately blamed all of the land settlers who lived in the area, instead of seeing the difference between those who were interested in farming and those who had actually invaded Motilone territory.

The land settlers retaliated by calling me a fake. I was in the jungle, and by the time I came out again for medical supplies, newspaper headlines were claiming that I was exploiting the Indians, making them mine gold and diamonds for me. I laughed. I could picture myself lounging in a high-backed rattan chair, dressed in a white suit and panama hat, sipping a drink while Motilones waited on me.

I talked to Dr. Landinez about it. "What should I do?" I asked.

"Listen," he said, "don't do a thing. It's just natural that there'll be a lot of talk. The Motilones are a fascinating group, and no one has any way of proving or disproving anything that's said about them. You do your work, be honest with the Indians, and let everyone think what he wants to think. If you spend time worrying about what people think of you, you'll never get anything done."

So I went back into the jungle. Interest in the Motilones continued, but since there wasn't any way of getting information about them, the whole affair quieted down.

Then, in 1970, a government commission was flown into the area in a helicopter to solve boundary problems between Colombia and Venezuela. They were surprised to find, at one communal home, a health center and a school staffed by Motilones. Newspaper accounts hadn't prepared them for anything like that. They managed to ask the Motilones who had been responsible—a difficult task, since they didn't speak Motilone.

Naturally the Motilones said, "Bruchko."

That proved I was a fake. The real hero of the Motilone development, the papers wrote, was someone named "Bruchko."

A few months later another commission came into the region by helicopter. Fortunately, they talked to a Motilone who had learned some Spanish.

"We want to see Olson," the Commissioner said.

"We not know Olson," the Motilone said in broken Spanish.

The Commissioner was surprised. "Olson doesn't live here?"

"No," the Motilone said, shaking his head. "Motilones live here."

"Olson, a tall, blond fellow?"

"Oh, Bruchko!"

From that time on, we had favorable publicity. Favorable publicity, however, doesn't cure sick people. It doesn't fill hungry mouths. It doesn't guarantee that no one will try to run you out of your family home. All it seemed to do was guarantee hostility with many of the land settlers.

At about this time there was a major prison break in Colombia. Many of the escapees came into the wild colonial areas near Motilone territory, because they would be left alone there. They began to farm and, of course, saw the Motilones as a threat both to their control of the area and to their freedom from government forces, since the Motilones were happy to cooperate with the Colombian government.

Resentment built up, even though many bandits received medical attention from Motilones. The regular land settlers went back and forth in their allegiance. They didn't like the bandits. But then, they resented the fact that the newspapers had cast them as villains in the struggle for land. And it was true that they wanted to get at the Motilone lands. Often their sympathies were with the bandits. Some open hostility developed.

Contact with the outside world, which totally destroyed the culture of many primitive tribes, certainly was a threat to the Motilones. It was a threat they would have to face. I could only pray that, when the time came, they would be strong in Jesus Christ to resist anyone who tried to change their customs.

For myself, at least one precious thing came from the contact with the outside world. Gloria. Her brother, a lieutenant in the Colombian army, was in charge of the military outpost in Tibu. A husky, tall fellow, he was interested in the jungle, though he'd never spent time there. When he got a vacation, he planned to go as far into the jungle as he could. I had met him several times in Tibu, and tried to discourage him. He seemed to think that the jungle was some kind of lovely state park that you might picnic in. It wasn't easy to convince him otherwise.

I met Gloria in 1965 after a particularly hard trip out to Tibu. Because I was in a hurry to get medicine for the Motilones, I didn't stop to hunt for food. And on the whole trip I didn't happen to see anything I could eat. I just kept going. Nor did I get much water to drink.

It was a mistake. I began to feel weak. On the third night on the trail I was so exhausted I had to stop early. I knew I needed food, but I couldn't even get up to look for any. I fell into a fitful sleep.

I dreamed about the jungle. It was beautiful and green and filled with butterflies. One flew into my mouth and got stuck, because its wings were wet. I could feel it beat its wings and struggle to get out. I half woke up. I was groggy.

There's a butterfly in my mouth. How strange, I thought. *I'd better take it out.*

I put my hand in my mouth—and I *did* grab something. I started pulling it out. The more I pulled, the more came out.

Then I really woke up. I could feel this thing struggling all the way out of my throat. When I got it out and looked at it, I felt sick to my stomach.

It was an intestinal worm, about a foot and a half long. He had gotten so hungry he had crawled up my throat looking for food.

From that experience I learned to always eat something

on the trail, if only to keep the parasites happy.

The next day I took time to hunt some food, and a few days later arrived in Tibu, feeling exhausted. There I met Gloria. She was studying law in Bogota, and had come down to visit her brother for a few days. Slender and pretty, she was wearing jeans and a leather jacket. Her black hair was tied into a pony tail. I didn't pay much attention to her, since I was in a hurry to get back with the medicine.

Her brother, however, hadn't given up his idea about seeing the jungle. He had five days furlough coming up, and wanted me to take him and Gloria with me. I was eating a meal with them when he popped the question. I looked over at Gloria. She was looking down at her plate.

"I don't think you understand," I said. "The jungle is not a picnic ground."

Gloria's head shot up. "I do understand," she said. "Whatever gave you the idea you were the only one who could survive in it?"

I sputtered at that, "The jungle is no place for women. You wouldn't last two days on the trail."

"Try me," she said.

I got a little angry. "All right," I said. "You can come as long as you keep up. But I don't have the time to play nursemaid. If you don't keep up, you go back. By yourselves."

The next morning, when we were getting ready to leave, I realized it was foolish to try to take them back to the Motilone home I had come from. So, instead, I took them to the Motilone home nearest Tibu. It was a two-day trip by boat. When I saw how game they were, I was ashamed of myself for not showing them how tough the jungle really could be.

We reached the communal home on a fishing day. The dams already had been built, and the men were beginning to spear the fish, charging up and down the river, yelling and splashing. Gloria wanted to join them. I had to laugh. I got her a spear. She went into the water up to her waist, and walked downriver, peering beneath the surface like a pro. Half an hour later she came back, dripping wet, smiling, with a big fish dangling from her spear. The Motilones loved her for it. No other woman had ever gone fishing, let alone speared a large fish.

That night we sat around the fire inside the communal home, and told stories about the Motilones. One of the Motilone women came up to Gloria, felt her long hair and complimented her on it. Then she smiled and said, "Are you Bruchko's wife?"

I blushed, and Gloria wanted to know what she had asked. I said she had asked whether she was a young woman. It was all I could think of.

"It's obvious that I'm a young woman," Gloria replied, laughing. "What did she really ask?"

I blushed again and refused to tell her, but the two of them teased me until I did. "She wanted to know whether you are my wife."

She looked at her brother, and they smiled. "Yeah," she said.

It was a wonderful week. Gloria helped the women weave and do all their work. She was infatuated with the Motilone way of life and the Motilones loved her.

When the week was up, Gloria stood in the middle of the clearing and swung her arm around, indicating all of it.

"What can I do?" she asked.

"What do you mean?"

"I mean, what can I do? How can I help?"

I didn't take her seriously. Everyone wants to help.

"You can study to be a doctor," I said flippantly, "and come in here and help with the health facilities."

I didn't see her again for five years, and I must say that I had quite thoroughly forgotten her. We had written a few letters, then, largely because of me, they had ended.

In 1970 I was in Bogota, walking down one of the busy streets, when someone poked a book into my back. I turned around. It was Gloria. She was the same girl I remembered, but she looked older, more mature.

"Where've you been?" she asked, with a teasing smile.

"In the jungle, of course," I said.

"Why didn't you write me?"

"Who has time to write? I've been busy."

"Nobody is that busy."

We started down the street. I asked her how her law studies were going. She stopped and nearly cried.

"What's the matter?" I asked, thinking maybe she had flunked out of law school and was ashamed.

"I'm in medical school now," she said. "You told me that if I wanted to help the Motilones I should go to medical school. I quit law school."

I could barely remember having told her, the advice had been so casual. But I suddenly realized that she was serious about helping the Motilones.

From then on, whenever I was in Bogota, I stopped to see her and her mother. (Her father had died years before.) Gloria and I would go to a Hungarian restaurant that we both liked, and would drink coffee and talk by the hour. When I couldn't go to Bogota I would talk to her on the radio—mostly about the Motilones. We also talked about Jesus.

Gloria was excited that the Gospel had given the Motilones hope, but she wasn't sure how that applied to her.

"My ideas aren't the same as those of the Motilones," she said one day while we were in a little cafe. "I can't understand Jesus. I don't feel I can really know Him."

"But can't you see how wonderful He is?" I asked. "Can't you see how much He loves you?"

She shook her head violently. "I can identify with His sufferings. I've suffered. I saw my father and my brother both die, and I think I know the feel of death. But Jesus— He rose again. Isn't that right? He rose again. I can't rise from my sufferings."

She put her head down on the table. I put my hand out and held it against her neck.

"You can," I said. "I don't know exactly how. It's always different. But you can rise. Anyone who wants to can, because God will do it for you and with you."

She just kept her head on the table and didn't say anything.

Later we went to one of the cathedrals in Bogota. In the middle of the mass Gloria, who had been praying, suddenly threw her arms around me and gave me a big kiss. She was crying. "How wonderful! How wonderful He is!" she said.

A lady next to us was quite concerned. "What's the matter?" she asked.

I laughed. "Nothing's wrong," I said. "We're just worshipping God."

Not long afterwards Gloria's mother also met Jesus, and there was quite a family scene, with both of them crying and hugging each other while I looked on, feeling a little embarrassed.

Gloria was going to graduate from medical school. In Colombia young doctors have to give one year of free medical service in the rural regions. I knew the Minister of Health in Colombia, and I asked him if there was a way for Gloria to serve for a year in Tibu, at a small home that had been established there for Motilones who needed more medical attention than they could get from the health centers in the communal homes.

"I'm sorry, Bruce," he said, "there's no possibility that we could send a single woman there. It's just too rough an area."

I stood still for a second. It seemed as though the air around me and the cars on the street outside and even the world also stood still. It was quiet a moment. Then I knew, and it was easy to say it.

"That won't be a problem. We're going to get married."

I think I was more surprised to hear myself say those words than she was later when I asked her.

22

Almost Wiped Out

I was staying in Tibu, working on the house that Gloria and I would stay in, enjoying thoughts of living there with her, and getting pleasure from the work of carpentering and roofing. Then word came from one of the Motilone homes that there was a widespread sickness that the witch doctors weren't able to treat. I took all the drugs that I was able to beg or borrow and left the next day.

I reached the home several days later. No one came out into the sunny clearing to greet me. Inside the house I could hear groanings and crying. I stooped and entered the door.

Bodies were everywhere. The only sign that they were alive was the constant groaning and wailing that, once inside the house, seemed like a madman's chant. There was an incredible stench that made my stomach flip-flop.

I ran from one person to the next, recognizing friends, unable to stop and help any one person because the moment I stopped to help, a groan would pull me toward another person. People were lying in their own vomit, unable to clean themselves. Their dung was scattered around their hammocks. Some had fallen out of their hammocks and were lying on the ground in their dung.

I began to clean those who were most dirty, and give medicine. I would no sooner get a man clean than he would have a bowel movement or would retch and my work would be undone. I would try to give pills, and they'd be sprayed back in my face. In no time my clothes and skin were stiff with dried vomit.

Most of the people there had been without food and water for five days or more, so one of the most immediate dangers was dehydration. Their skin was loose on their bodies. Because they couldn't drink without vomiting, the worst cases had to have intravenous feedings.

The first night I did not sleep at all. I craved sleep; but I couldn't lie down while people were near death. I kept moving, my legs and feet aching, wanting to collapse under me.

The next day Bobby came with several other men. Among them was my old friend Adjibacbayra, the chief who had challenged Bobby to the song at the Festival of the Arrows where the Motilones had first heard about Jesus. I put my hands on their shoulders, welcoming them. It had been as though I was the only living person in a world of ghosts.

There were signs of improvement that day. The drugs and the IV feedings were taking effect. And having others to work with us was heartening. As it got dark inside the house, I began to look forward to sleeping. When we lit fires and worked in the flickering light, the idea became an obsession. The only thing that helped keep me moving was the idea that I soon would be done.

But the hours dragged on, every minute painful as a knife.

Time and again I set myself a limit. "At ten o'clock I'll quit." But ten o'clock would pass, and there would be more that had to be done.

I reached my final limit at two o'clock in the morning. There was a momentary lull in the sickness, and I stood up and looked for Bobby. He walked over to me.

"Let's sleep," he said, and my heart said, *Oh, yes!* "And

then at five o'clock I think we had better start for Iquia-corara."

My mind didn't register, "Iquiacorara?"

"Yes," he said. "It's as bad as this."

"Bobby," I said, "you mean this isn't the only home?"

"Oh, no," he said. "All the homes in the lowland areas have got the sickness. They're not all as bad as this, but they're pretty bad."

I closed my eyes, and the darkness seemed to whirl inside my eyelids. More sickness. More vomit. Maybe some had already died. *Oh, Lord, deliver me.*

The next thing I knew I was being shaken awake. I opened my eyes to find myself lying in a hammock with Bobby leaning over me. I shut my eyes again.

"You've got to get up, Bruchko," Bobby said. "We've got to go to Iquiacorara."

I dragged myself out of the hammock.

We took no time to wash. Bobby already had told several of the men and women who were recovered enough to get up and move around what they should do to help the others. Then we left.

The worst of the epidemic went on for three weeks. During that time I never got more than two or three hours of sleep in twenty-four hours. Seven hundred people were treated for measles or their aftereffects.

Miraculously, only one person died—a little girl. When I first saw her I was with Adjibacbayra. She had shrunk to the size of a baby from dehydration. Adji put his hand out and touched her skin. It hung loose like rubber. He squeezed a little of it into a fold, and it stayed in that shape when he took his hand away. Two days later, despite everything we did, she died.

That night I couldn't go to bed. I was full of anger. I had to walk, to move. I started for another communal home, alone. I must have been half delirious, because I didn't feel tired. My anger burned like a fuel, forcing my sagging legs to move.

Coming up a hill, I saw a pair of eyes directly ahead, gleaming yellow. I thought it was a frog, since a certain kind of frog had eyes that color. Then I realized that the eyes were too far apart. So maybe there were two frogs.

Then I heard a hiss. The eyes moved. I saw a long, sleek, form move slightly. It was a panther, the first I'd ever seen.

I stopped. All my anger transferred itself to the cold, steady eyes of that animal. I hated him. I groped around my foot and found a stick. I took it and ran at the panther, screaming. He growled, and crouched. Then, when I was about ten feet from him, he turned and, in a quick, quiet hop, was gone.

I stood, yelling after him. Then I realized what I had done. My heart began to beat fast, and I suddenly was afraid that he would come back. "Thank you, Lord," I breathed into the darkness.

The next day I left the jungle. We needed more drugs, and the epidemic had subsided enough so that I wouldn't be missed. There were enough Motilones working under Bobby to keep up.

For a week and a half I fought paperwork and credit ratings instead of panthers, and wasn't sure which I preferred. I tried to get funds from the Colombian government, and to borrow money from anyone I could reach. When I thought I had gotten all I could, I went back to the jungle.

I found Adjibacbayra near death. Because we had worked side by side for three weeks, I had assumed that he had a natural resistance to the disease. But he not only had contracted the disease, but had gotten pneumonia as a by-product. He couldn't eat. Two days after I reached him he slipped into a coma. His body was yellow, and flies were crawling across his chest where his vomit had hardened. His face was covered with little blue dots from the rash. It was a horrible predicament for the man who had been strong enough to sing the Song of the Arrows for fourteen hours when God's Spirit had swept through the Motilones.

While I watched him, he blinked and woke up. I leaned over. His face was like a painted mask, lined and creased by pain.

"Bruchko," he said, "my body hurts. I hurt everywhere."

"Shh," I said. "You need to be quiet. We want you to be well. We want you to be strong."

He shook his head, barely moving it. "No, Bruchko.

I'm not well and I'm not strong. I have closed my eyes."

His eyes did close, and he slipped off. I stayed near him. Later he opened his eyes again.

"Bruchko, I heard a voice like the spirits that talk when they try to kill you."

I nodded.

"But this voice called me by my secret name, by my real name. No one alive knows my real name, but this spirit called me by my real name. So I called to it and said, "Who are you?' and it said, 'I am Jesus, who has walked with you on the trail.' "

Several other men gathered around him, including Atrara, the father of the little girl who had died.

"So I told Jesus that I hurt all over, from my head to my toes. And Jesus said that he wants me to come home."

His breath was coming with difficulty.

"Help me, brother!" he whispered, looking at me. "Help me!" Then he turned his eyes away. "But you can't," he said, "I've been embraced by death. I'm leaving. Bruchko, I'm leaving. I can't see. There's only pain. God is here and He wants to take me on the path we couldn't ever find on our hunts, the path that goes beyond the horizon to His home."

Then he smiled, and his face looked for a moment like the one I knew. "Not alone," he said. "Not alone. I won't walk it by myself. There's a Friend who wants to take me. And He knows my name, my *real* name."

Then his body sagged. He clutched my hand, and his fingers gradually went limp. I set his hand down beside his body and walked out of the home.

I stopped in the clearing. The sun was shining. How unbelievable. I walked into the jungle, where it was cool and dark, and I found a trail and began to walk it, without knowing or caring where it was going. Then I began to sing. I sang Adji's own song, the song he sang on the trail. I began by singing quietly under my breath, but soon I was bellowing out the tune at the top of my lungs, and I was crying.

"God," I sang, "I loved my brother, I long to sing his song with him again."

A hand touched my shoulder. I looked around, frightened. It was Atrara.

"Don't cry," he said. "Don't be sad. His language has walked beyond the horizon. It isn't lost in the jungles. You don't need to sing it here. It's gone to another place."

23

The Whirlpool

I woke up to the soft plip-plop of rain. The communal home was filled with soft early morning light, and everyone else was asleep. It must have rained all night, because no one had left to go hunting. I turned over in my hammock and went back to sleep.

I woke up again a few hours later. It was still raining.

That's odd, I thought. It almost never rains during the day in the jungle.

It had been several months since the measles epidemic. I had been relaxing, looking forward to marrying Gloria, and spending a lot of time with Bobby. I'd also been working on the linguistic materials I'd gathered during the ten years with the Motilones. There was interest in them among linguists, and I was planning to publish some papers about the Motilone language.

I decided to work on that. There wouldn't be much point in trying to do anything else as long as it was raining. I went down to the health center—a walk of about six

201

hundred yards. It was only drizzling, but there were puddles everywhere. I walked by the banana patch, and saw that the young trees were doing well. None had been knocked over by the wind. I slipped on the mud and fell, laughing. I couldn't remember when I had seen so much water.

At the health center, I sat down at the desk we had made by cutting a section out of a felled mahogany tree. That and a waterproof, insectproof file for my papers were my most precious possessions.

The water drummed pleasantly on the tin roof of the health center and I settled down to work. An hour or so later, I was disturbed by loud voices. I went to the door and looked out. Two Motilone men across the river were shouting for a canoe to bring them back. The canoe was filled with water, and had to be emptied out. Because the water was high from all the rain, it was some time before the men got across and back with the stranded men. I decided to go up to the home to hear what they had to say. I knew they were from an area not far from Tibu, and I thought they might have a message for me.

When I got to the home everyone was watching them eat. They had been on the trail for several days, and were tired and hungry. They were laughing about some of the things that had happened to them. Evidently, it had been rough going. A lot of trees had been blown down, and some of the rivers had been difficult to cross. I squatted down to listen. A few minutes later Bobby came in. I waved to him and smiled. The two men talked about the hunting they had been doing, and one of them told a funny story about stubbing his toe on the trip. Bored, I got up to leave. They had nothing but small talk. I walked back down to the health center and began to write again.

About an hour later I looked up to see the two men standing in the door. They handed me a little packet of five envelopes.

"Where did these come from?" I asked.

They shrugged "George Camiyocbayra gave them to us to give to you." George was in charge of procurement in Tibu.

"Thanks," I said.

They were telegrams. I opened the first. "She is buried," it said.

Who was buried? It must be Gloria's mother. But no, her mother had sent it. She had signed it at the bottom.

I ripped open the others. Gloria had been in an accident. Her car had flipped over the edge of a cliff. "Come at once," one of the telegrams said. "We're waiting for you. You must come immediately." But it was dated two weeks before. Another telegram said that Gloria had died and that her funeral would be in three days.

I threw the telegrams down and ran to the house. Bobby was making arrows. He looked up at me with the same sweet smile he'd had as a boy.

"Bobby," I choked out, "she isn't coming. She won't be coming here."

"What?" he said.

"She isn't coming, Bobby. Gloria isn't coming. She died. She's dead."

Another Motilone came into the home and put his hand on my shoulder, not knowing I was upset. I shook him off.

"How do you know she's dead?" Bobby asked.

"The writing said so. Those letters that came today from Tibu.

"Bobby," I said, "I've got to go to Bogota. We've got to go right now."

"Sure, sure," he said. "When the water goes down we'll go."

That was a long day. Sometimes the sadness was more than I could take. Other times it was unreal. I couldn't believe that it had really happened. I read the telegrams again and again. Bobby talked and sang to me, telling about Gloria, remembering how she had been the first foreign woman ever to come into the Motilone region, recalling how she had speared fish.

My mind went over and over Gloria's death like a machine that won't stop working. I couldn't cry, and I couldn't pray, though I tried. But pray for what? She was dead. She'd been dead for weeks.

That night I lit a candle and lay in my hammock listening to the rain. It had continued all that day, and now was coming down in buckets. Suddenly I knew I had to get out of there. I had to go to Bogota. I had to at least see Gloria's grave and talk to her mother. If I didn't, I would never really know that it wasn't a bad dream.

I tossed back and forth all night, waiting for it to get light. At three o'clock in the morning I got up and shook Bobby. "Bobby, I want to go out now, I've got to go to Bogota. I think it's getting light, and we can travel."

He told me to go back to bed. It was still dark, and it was raining. Then it began to really pour. I prayed for it to stop. I heard the sound of the river rushing over rocks and boulders, then it quieted and I realized it was over its banks. When it got light, the water was a good twelve feet over flood stage, and only six feet from the home.

But I *had* to get downriver. It was a compulsion.

"Bobby," I said, "let's go!"

"Bruchko, we can't. We'll drown."

"But you're a good pilot, Bobby. I know you could get us down."

He shook his head. "It's impossible. The river is too high."

I wasn't asking him, I was telling him. He finally agreed, sadly. I packed my linguistic materials in their watertight packet, and corralled the two baby wild bears I wanted to send to a friend in the U.S. At about ten in the morning we finally got off. Although the river had dropped about four feet from its crest, it still was high, brown and ugly, with sucking swirls of yellow foam around the rocks. Bobby was worried.

"Are you sure you have to do this, Bruchko?" he asked. "The river is just too high to make it."

I didn't respond. I just kept packing the canoe.

We finally set out, Bobby and I and two other men. Still other Motilones came down from the house and stood in the rain, saying good-bye.

"When you see Gloria's mother tell her that my stomach aches for her," Atacadara, Bobby's wife, said. "Tell her that when we heard Gloria was dead, we couldn't eat. We know how she feels."

I took a last glance at the home and got in the canoe.

We gave the boat a push, and the water picked us up and pulled us downstream.

There was no fighting the current, even with the outboard motor on the canoe. All we could do was steer away from the bad spots. Bobby's face was tense. He knew the river better than any other person alive, but not even he could anticipate the logs when the muddy water was going at twice its normal speed.

Suddenly a huge tree trunk rolled up alongside us, on our left. We watched it closely to make sure it didn't wheel around and hit us. As we came into a bend in the river, I realized that there was a whirlpool to the right of us. The log would push us into it if we weren't careful.

"Bobby, look out ahead!" I yelled. But he was leaning over the motor. The nylon thread that controlled the throttle had broken, and he was trying to tie it.

Then another log came surging up out of the bottom of the river. It hit the big trunk on our left, bouncing it into our boat with a jolt that knocked us straight toward the whirlpool. Bobby tried to cut the motor, to slow the boat and get away from the log. There wasn't time. We could see the whirlpool, very close and twice its normal size. Bobby tried to swing the boat around and go against the current, but the current was too strong. The canoe hit the eye of the whirlpool sideways. It whirled about, then flipped over. We were all thrown out. I saw the gasoline tanks floating on the water. I had my papers in my hands, and the two baby bears under one arm. I wanted to grab onto the boat to hold myself up, so I let the bears go. They immediately started swimming, and I grabbed the boat with one hand and held my papers up with the other.

Then I saw Bobby swimming in the eye of the whirlpool. Without a splash, he was pulled down and disappeared. I couldn't see anything but the sloppy cone of dirty water. Then the canoe got closer to the whirlpool and started moving faster. All this time we were going around and around. Suddenly I was tossed off the boat and had to tread water. I was still holding my papers. The water took me around in a circle once, then again, pulling me closer to its eye. There was no avoiding it.

On the third time around I saw a tree limb stretched over

the water. I wondered why I hadn't noticed it before. I reached out my free arm and grabbed it. It was solid. Then I looked up and saw one of the Motilone men at the end of it. He pulled me out of the water, hand over hand, and I crawled up on the bank, in the mud, gasping for air. Oh, praise God!

But where was Bobby? Then I realized what I had done by insisting on this crazy trip! Bobby was dead.

"Did you see Bobby?" I asked frantically.

"No. He disappeared into the whirlpool."

I told the men I would jump into the river and float down until I found Bobby. But they said I couldn't, the river would suck me in and I would die.

A cliff bordered the river at this point, and we couldn't get downriver without scaling it, so we began to scramble up. I was frantic. I fell down and cut my finger.

I've got to find Bobby, I said to myself.

I left the papers and kept climbing. Again I fell and got a long gash in my leg. When I reached the top, I got a thorn in my bare feet. It went in over an inch, and I had to stop for the pain. *All hell has been let loose against me,* I thought. But I dragged on as soon as I could stand it, and looked out over the river, scanning the banks.

I saw the canoe, like a fat needle along the bank. Then I saw Bobby holding onto it. Oh, God! I ran down the hill, falling over the rocks. I reached Bobby and helped him pull in the canoe, then helped him out of the water. I placed my hand on his shoulder.

"I thought you were dead," he said.

"I thought you were dead," I said.

He was completely naked: the whirlpool had ripped off all his clothes. "Look," he said, "I lost all the clothes I was going to wear in civilization, and my money was in them."

"Who cares?" I said. "You're alive. Praise Jesus!"

Then the other two men came up. I was so relieved, I couldn't say much. I smiled and touched them all. Then we bailed out the canoe and continued downriver.

The rest of the trip went without incident. When we were a few miles from the Rio de Oro, we stopped beside the river. Bobby made a G-string out of a big leaf, and we went into town.

When I got on the airplane for Tibu, Bobby put his hand on my shoulder. "Tell Gloria's mother that we're hungry for her, that we're all sad that Gloria died," he said. "Take care of yourself, and come back soon."

"I will," I promised.

24

Beyond the Horizon

I went first to Bogota and spent three days with Gloria's mother. The close call on the trip downriver had given me some perspective on my grief. I had lost Gloria. But I still had Bobby.

Instead of going back to Tibu, I flew to the United States to discuss this book. I was there three weeks. When I returned to South America, Bobby met me in Tibu. I was sick of civilization and glad to be back in the jungle.

But civilization still needled me. The outlaws in the region were plotting to force the Motilones farther out of their territory. On our trip upriver we were threatened by Humberto Abril. I tried to dismiss it, but his words kept repeating themselves in my mind.

"For this cross, I'll kill you," he had said. They were such strange words, cold and chilling.

More threats followed by letter—not only to me, but to Bobby. One letter informed him that all the Motilones would have to get out because they (the outlaws) were going to take over the land. They threatened force.

The next day Humberto Abril's associate, Graciano, and five other people arrived in Iquiacorora in a canoe. I met him at the bank of the river.

"Who are those people?" I asked.

"They're sick and need medical attention," he said. "One of them is pretty badly infected. The others need one thing or another, so they came along.

"Oh yes," he added, "I brought you a letter, too." He handed it me, then walked up to the health center with the others.

I got out my knife and cut open the envelope. The letter was from Abril.

"Get out of here," it said. "This land is for colonization, and we're going to kill you. Any Indian that gives resistance will be rubbed out."

Thoroughly angry, I charged up the hill to the health center. I stuck the letter in Graciano's face.

"Read it," I commanded.

He shook his head. "I don't read."

"Well then, I'll read it for you." I read it out loud.

"Just how gullible do you think we are?" I asked. "You threaten us with death, yet you expect us to cheerfully cure your people. Now get your treatment, then get out of here. And don't bother to come back."

I threw the letter on the ground and pressed it into the mud with my shoe.

The Motilone leaders came to me that night to discuss the problem.

"We've decided that we'll fight if they try force," they told me. We're preparing for it now. We intend to get some guns and to use them and our arrows to defend the home."

They asked me what I thought.

"I don't think anything," I said. "I stand behind whatever you decide, as always."

Two tension-filled months went by. More threats were made, particularly against the Motilones who had built small homes along the river.

Bobby and I worked on the translation of Philippians. It was one of the most intense, most wonderful times of translation we had ever had together. Our minds were preoccupied with death, it seemed, because of the inevitable conflict with the colonists. And Philippians spoke to us about this death!

As we worked through the first chapter, we came to verse twenty where Paul says that his great expectation is that he will not be put to shame, but that Christ will be exalted in him whether in life or death.

I needed the right word for expectation. A Motilone expects to go to bed at night, but that word doesn't have much force.

The center of emotion for a Motilone is in his stomach. To have a full stomach is to have a happy heart. What was the surest way of having a full stomach? Probably to have hunted and killed a large tapir. You eat tapir until you can't eat any more.

So I took the verb for having a tapir in your possession, and I invented a new tense: I put it in a future tense that has already been completed, then I made it superlative.

I gave Bobby the word. It shocked him. "No," he said, "that's too big a word. It's too forceful. How can you expect something as much as that?"

We let it drop, but it must have bothered Bobby. Two or three days later he said, "Bruchko, let's go back to that word."

"All right," I said.

He was quiet for a while, thinking, then said, "Bruchko, is Jesus Christ that expectation for you in your life? Really?"

That stopped me short. It's one thing to figure out the right word to use, it's quite another thing to be asked if it's true of your own life. I thought of my conversion, and of some of the crises I had weathered with the Yukos and the Motilones. Finally, after a long silence, I said, "Yes."

Then I nodded vigorously. "Yes, Bobby. With all my strength and all my will I want to give myself to the expectation of Jesus Christ."

Bobby looked down at his feet. "Yes," he said. "It's a good word."

"Are you sure?" I asked.

He nodded.

Continuing with the translation we came to the part where Paul says he wants to be conformed to the image of Jesus Christ, through his own suffering or through his death. Bobby took the same powerful grammatical construction we had just used—something already done, yet lying in the future, in a superlative form—and applied it to the verb for conformity to Christ.

"*I'll* be completed in conformity to Christ's death," he said.

I felt burdened, as though I were carrying both my weight and Bobby's. What had I done? I had brought Jesus to the Motilones, yes; but was I ready to bring them this kind of conformity—conformity to the death of Christ? Had I brought death as well as life? I was eager to pray. Bobby was even more eager. But Bobby's prayer sent chills down my back.

"Christ Jesus, I want to be conformed to Your image. You *are* my expectation."

In the danger-charged atmosphere, that prayer seemed audacious. Bobby was saying, *I don't care whether I live or whether I die; I want to be like Jesus.* He was giving his life away.

For the next three weeks everything was quiet. We waited to hear from the outlaws, but no word came. Perhaps it had been a game, a useless threat that never would be carried out.

Bobby had to go downriver to sell some bananas. He took two other Motilones with him. He was expected back by four o'clock the following day. The river was at its normal height; the canoe was in good condition and there was no reason why he should be delayed. But four o'clock came, than five o'clock, and still no sign of Bobby. I began to be concerned. I had hated to see him go at all. Now my mind was full of all the things that might have happened to him. Six o'clock came. The sun went down. Only the river shone faintly in the dusk. Night noises began to rise out of the jungle. They were so ordinary a part of life that I usually hardly noticed them, but that night each one seemed foreboding.

At six-thirty Abacuriana, Asrayda, George Camiyoc-bara and I got into a canoe to go downriver to look for

Bobby and his canoe. The others weren't eager to go. It isn't easy to travel at night on the river. There was no moon, and rocks could appear in the path of our boat with no warning at all. After going through the first rapids, the canoe was swamped with water. We bailed out and continued. On the next rapids, we scraped our propeller against a rock but managed to clear it and continue on our way.

As we rounded a bend in the river, another canoe suddenly materialized out of the gloom. We nearly hit it. I threw the beam of my flashlight on it, and saw Aniano Buitrago, one of Humberto Abril's men, and some of his cohorts. I didn't call out to them, but kept my flashlight in their eyes so they couldn't recognize us. In a moment the river had whisked us by them. But what were they doing on the river at night?

A little farther down we passed another canoe going upriver. It was filled with more outlaws. Our flashlight beam probed the shore, as we looked for Bobby or his canoe. There was no sign of him.

Two more canoes passed us going upriver, filled with men I didn't know. Then we drifted by one of the land settler's homes. At least ten canoes were tied to the dock. The night seemed alive with threats.

Then George whispered, "Look! Isn't that Bobby's canoe?" He was pointing at the dock. I strained to see, but couldn't tell. We floated on by. It couldn't have been Bobby's. He wouldn't stop at one of the settler's homes, especially when Saphadana, a small Motilone home, was located only a few hundred yards farther downriver.

We considered going back for a second look.

"No," I said. "Let's go down to Saphadana and ask Aystoicana if he's seen Bobby."

We stopped the canoe on the bank near the communal home. There was no fire going inside, no sound.

Then I heard a Motilone voice. "Bruchko?"

"Yes."

Aystoicana came running down to the bank. I could barely see his face.

"Bruchko, they've killed Bobarishora. He's dead."

I couldn't grasp what he had said. "That's impossible!" I replied. "We're expecting him in Iquiacarora. Has he passed by here?"

Aystoicana grabbed my arm. "Bruchko, listen to me. Bobby's dead. He's been murdered."

Stunned, I fell onto my knees on the beach. "Where are the two men who were with him?"

"I don't know," he said. "They were badly hurt. They've gone."

I reached out and grabbed Aystoicana's knee, steadying myself. The night seemed covered with red and blue blotches, like wounds. "What happened?" I whispered.

"Bobby was with Satayra and Akasara. They were coming upriver, passing by Israel's farm. Israel was on the bank, motioning and calling them to come over. Bobby was late. He didn't want to stop, but since he'd known Israel for a long time, he thought it might be an emergency."

"Israel was up for treatment two or three times in the last few months," I said hoarsely. "He had a broken arm that I sewed up and set for him. And he got the drugs he needed from us."

"Yes," Aystoicana said. "So Bobby thought he was a friend. He took the canoe over to the bank. While he was leaning over the motor to turn it off, Satayra looked up and saw a man standing behind a tree with a shotgun.

"Satayra yelled to Bobby and Akasara, telling them to jump into the river. Bobby didn't hear because he was too close to the motor. Satayra jumped up on the bank and grabbed for the shotgun. As he wrestled with the man for the gun, the man reached for his machete. Satayra let go of the gun to protect himself, and the man used his machete to slit Satayra's arm open from the wrist to the elbow. Satayra tumbled into the river, and Akasara jumped out of the boat to protect himself.

"Bobby tried to get out of the boat but a blast from the shotgun caught him in the groin. He fell into the river. Some of the pellets hit Akasara in the leg, but he and Satayra swam to the other side of the river. They looked for Bobby, but all they could see was red in the water. Then they saw his body floating. They also saw swarms of colonists on the other bank. All had guns. They had been waiting for Bobby. Akasara and Satayra were frightened and ran. They came here and told us."

"Oh, no, no; oh, no," I whispered.

A Motilone whistled in the distance. Since their language is tonal, the Motilones don't always use words. This whistling said that two canoes were floating downstream. There was no sound of motors. I realized that whoever was in them was trying to be quiet. They must be enemies.

"I want to go downriver to get the military," I said, suddenly angry. "George, you come with me."

I got into the boat. As I pulled the cord to start the motor, I heard little zinging noises on the water. They were shotgun pellets—fired from too great a distance to do any damage. The motor started on the third try and we quickly left the gunshots behind.

It took several hours to reach the Rio de Oro military station. I woke up the commander of the armed forces. He came downstairs in his pajamas. I told him there had been a plot to kill Bobarishora, and that he was reported to be dead.

He listened to my story, staring in space with sleep-glazed eyes. "Okay, I'll check into it," he said, and opened the door for me to leave.

"I don't want you to check into it," I said. "I want some help now. I need somebody to protect the Motilones."

"Sorry," he said. "I can't do anything tonight."

I went to the police. They wouldn't do anything either. I don't think they were unconcerned about the problem. They were afraid of being attacked themselves.

I was angry and frustrated. At four in the morning I started back upriver with George. Dawn was just beginning to break. A pearly gray light on the water got brighter as we went upstream. The foliage took on a lush green color. It all looked so innocent. These were the trees and the river that I loved. This was home.

Bobby couldn't be dead. I refused to believe it. I kept thinking about the time a few months before when our boat had been pulled into the whirlpool. I had thought Bobby was dead then. But he had survived. Miraculously, he might even now be in the jungle, waiting for help, staying out of the outlaws' sight.

When we reached Saphadana the sun was shining. It

didn't seem possible that we could have been shot at there. But Aystoicana told us that the settlers and outlaws had been coming by all night, shooting into Motilone homes near the river, and shouting that the Motilones had to leave, that the land no longer belonged to them.

"Have you looked for Bobby?" I asked.

"We've looked, but we haven't found a trace."

"We've got to look," I said. "He may need our help. He may be wounded in the jungle."

Aystoicana looked down at his feet, as though a little embarrassed. We spent the whole day in the jungle, hunting for Bobby. The others wanted to quit, but I wouldn't let them.

I had not slept in a day and a half, and was at the end of my strength. Sometimes my voice would fade, and there would be nothing but the sound of the birds singing faintly in the trees. There was never an answer from Bobby.

At five o'clock we quit. It would be dark by the time our canoe reached Saphadana. We didn't talk; we were too tired, too sick.

When we reached the point where the Cano Tomas River comes into the Rio de Oro, I saw something floating in the river. It looked like a log. We went over to investigate. It was Bobby, face down.

All hope drained out of my body. I felt empty—like a shell. I had convinced myself that this would be like the time we had nearly drowned. Bobby would be alive. We would be reunited.

The river was shallow. I got out of the canoe and turned Bobby over. His face, stark white, was crinkly from being in the water. I closed his eyes with my fingers. He had died at once. The shotgun blast had ripped open the lower half of his body.

"God," I cried, "oh, God, why?"

He had been the leader of his people, the first to know Christ, the first to read and to build schools, the first to take a stand against the thieves of civilization.

George handed me a blanket. I wrapped it around Bobby's body, then helped lift him into our canoe.

The next day we took his body to Iquiacarora. My mind wouldn't let me rest. I had cried that night until no more tears would come. Still my thoughts went in circles. *Why all this death, Lord,* I kept asking. The river was death. The jungle was death. Death flowed down the valleys. Always it touched someone I loved . . . Gloria . . . Bobby. And woven through my thoughts were the chilling words of Humberto: "For this cross I'll kill you!"

The river was low, and we had to spend a lot of time getting through the shallow areas. At one such place I heard the zip, zip of bullets hitting the water. They came from two canoes across the river. Suddenly a shot split the side of our canoe. We struggled frantically to get past the outlaws, but they were gaining on us.

I felt a burning shock in my leg. A bullet had hit me.

We finally got the canoe loose. As we started into the deeper water another bullet creased my chest. It actually felt good. I wanted to be hurt. I wanted pain. I wanted death.

But I received only surface wounds. We stopped the flow of blood; the pellets would have to be taken out later.

After many more hours of riding slowly upstream, we rounded the bend in the river that led to Iquiacorara. Several hundred Motilones were on the bank, armed. When they recognized us, they waited quietly until we disembarked. The news of Bobby's death had spread, and people had come from miles around. They crowded around the boat.

I saw Atacadara, Bobby's wife, standing above us on a little knoll. She was watching me, waiting. I looked at her, bowing my head to confirm that Bobby was dead. She turned and walked away, one of her little girls clinging to her leg. She had Bobby's youngest son in her arms.

We got my hammock from the home, and tied it to a twelve-foot pole. Lifting Bobby's body out of the boat, we put it in the hammock, then covered it with my blanket because he was my pact brother. Then we carried the hammock across the river and downstream, and hung it far up in the highest branches so the vultures could eat Bobby's body.

Returning, I found Atacadara standing by herself on the edge of the jungle. Her eyes were dark and empty, like they had been when her daughter had died.

She looked up at me, and I broke into tears.

She grabbed my shoulder. "No, no," she said. I held her for a little while, then let her go.

All day I sat outside the home and watched the vultures swoop out of the sky. They began as high dark specks. Circling closer with their huge unflapping wings, they landed in the trees with short, stuttering flaps.

I remembered when I had thought the ceremony cold and cruel; had thought sticking someone in a box and putting him in a hole was better than tying him high in a tree to be carried off into the sky. I knew now what it meant. It meant that Bobby was free to go beyond the horizon.

I only wished I could go with him.

Some Motilones tried to talk to me as I squatted outside the home, tried to cheer me. But I sat like stone.

That night I could stand it no longer. I went out into the jungle to the trees that held Bobby's hammock. There I would lay down to sleep under the hammock that held Bobby's body; to say a final goodbye. But when I went the whole home followed me. There were about two hundred people. We crossed the river together. It was dark under the hammock. There was no moon.

"Let's all hold hands in a circle that has no beginning and no ending, and let's talk to God," I said.

It wasn't according to Motilone culture, but it seemed the right thing to do.

Odo, Bobby's adopted son, was the first to pray. He was only fourteen, but God gave him the most beautiful, prophetic prayer I have ever heard.

"Oh, God," he said loudly, looking up at the silhouette of Bobby's hammock. "God, this is black, it's dark, I can't see. We're lost."

He was quiet for a moment, then continued in a new quieter voice. "God, there is a tree, a tall tree, with its roots going very deeply into the ground. It's us, Lord, it's the Motilone people.

"We've lived in this land all our lives, generation after generation, and our roots are very deep, and we stand tall.

"We tried to follow God, but we lost Him while we were

trying to follow. We tried to follow our own paths, and they never took us to the place they were supposed to; they only ended at another home, or at a river. They never took us beyond the horizon, where we would find You.

"Then Bobarishora found Your path in Jesus Christ, and he walked it, and showed us how to walk it. We were glad.

"But God! Where has it taken him? Why did that path lead to this place? God, it can't be."

He stopped. There was absolute silence.

"The tree is beautiful," he said. "It is beautiful. It is covered with large, perfect blossoms that have opened and shine in the sun. Each of us is a flower.

"But there is one flower bigger and more beautiful than all the rest, It made the most perfect fruit. That is Bobarishora. He gave us agriculture, and our stomachs were filled. We were dying of sickness, and he brought us healing from Jesus Christ through medicine. He showed us the path to walk with Jesus Christ, so that we have reasons for life, for living. We were all excited by this new life.

"But, oh Lord, it's so black. A wind has blown, and the fruit, the most perfect fruit, has dried and withered and fallen to the ground. Its seeds have been kicked into the dark, dark ground. It has died . . . . Bobarishora has died, and left us.

"God, don't let the seed be wasted. Make our lives fertile soil so that his seed may grow in us. Make his death into a great tree growing in our soil, so that we can live as he did, to help each other and learn to love. Make this grow up in us because of his death. We ask this because we are all one this evening, in a circle holding hands, born into Jesus Christ, Your only Son."

Our circle buckled and broke slowly apart. I saw something I had never seen among the Motilones before: people were hiding their eyes, and sniffling.

Ocdabidayna walked up to me, trying to smile. "Look at us all. Everybody has the flu!" he said.

"No," I said. "It's not the flu that I have. It's no flu."

Then Ocdabidayna, one of the leading chiefs, grabbed his head with his two hands and fell on the ground. "Oh,

Bruchko," he said, looking up at me, "I'm not a man. I'm a baby, a tiny baby. Only babies cry."

His agony shook the Motilones as I have never seen them shaken. They ran into the jungle to hide their own tears from each other.

"Bruchko," Ocdabidayna said. "Jesus Christ died for all the tribes of the world. Bobby is almost like Him. He died for the Motilones."

I spent the next three weeks recovering from my wounds. I wanted to get out of the jungle, to leave the smell of death. I also wanted to inform the right authorities of the outlaw situation. But I couldn't leave. The river was ambushed. Anyone who tried to make it out would have been killed. Hunters also found that the trails out of the jungle were booby-trapped with shotguns. One of the men did walk out to Tibu, carrying several letters. It took him a week, walking only at night, and always avoiding the trails.

The only sure way out was over the mountains—a journey requiring one-hundred-forty walking hours. My leg had healed, so I began the trip. When I had gone halfway I heard a helicopter. The President of Colombia had sent it for me. I was soon out of the jungle.

I spent a restless week in Bogota. What did it all mean? For the Motilones, Bobby might grow up into a flowering tree. But what meaning did the murder of my pact-brother have for me?

As I talked to one of the head ministers in the Colombian government one night, I got my answer. He had known Bobarishora personally, and had a great interest in the Motilone people. I had just described Bobby's death, and there were tears in his eyes.

"But Bruce," he said, "you keep talking as though you wished Jesus would intervene and put an end to all this trouble. Can't you see that it's just the opposite. If it weren't for Jesus, the Motilones would be pushed back into the jungle until they were slowly but surely eliminated! If it weren't for Jesus, there would be no struggle; Bobby would never have had to die like he did.

"No, Bruce. It's not in spite of Jesus that Bobby died. It's because of Jesus."

He put his hand on my shoulder. "Where would the Motilone people be if Bobby had not been the sort of person whom the bandits felt they had to kill? Where would *you* be if Bobby hadn't been that sort of person?"

"Nowhere," I said. "I'd be nowhere."

So life has to be like this, I thought. *It has to be struggling and crying, even dying.*

Suddenly I saw my parents, and all the pain we had gone through . . .

I saw the Yukos, and the faces of the settlers . . .

I saw the faces of the Motilones, for whom the rest of the New Testament still had to be translated.

There was so much to do . . . so many things that Christ had called me to do. It would take more pain, more loneliness. Maybe death.

Why was it so hard? Why?

Then I saw Jesus. He was struggling up a hill with a great burden. His face was lined with grief; His back bent.

I steadied myself on the back of a chair, and looked at the minister of government.

"I think I see," I said. "It's the cross."

I held up my hand, and put my thumb across my forefinger. "It's for this cross."